the

Punani Proverbs

Healing Practices For The Modern Womb

first edition

by Tahtahme

Intended for Ages 17+

THIS WORKBOOK IS NOT INTENDED FOR THE PURPOSE OF PROVIDING MEDICAL ADVICE

All information, content, and material of this workbook is for informational purposes only and are not intended to serve as a substitute for the consultation, diagnosis, and/or medical treatment of a qualified physician or healthcare provider.

This workbook is to be used as a tool
to aid you on your journey to come to know your own punani intimately,
unleash your creativity, heal, manifest,
trust in your power, know your worth, &
seduce with your punani in all the ways.

Note: *Be sure to show love to the rest of your body!*

Warning: Hoodoo and Rootwork are an African American Traditional Religion that is based upon prayer with African American Ancestors. The information pertaining to both Hoodoo and Rootwork contained within this book will only work exactly for people of the correct bloodline, and will need to be modified for other African Traditional Religion, and forsaken altogether by people who have no relation or legitimate connection.

"Melanin Monroe" Art on following page by Emani Delapina (facebook.com/emani.delapina). This painting was modified for the cover.

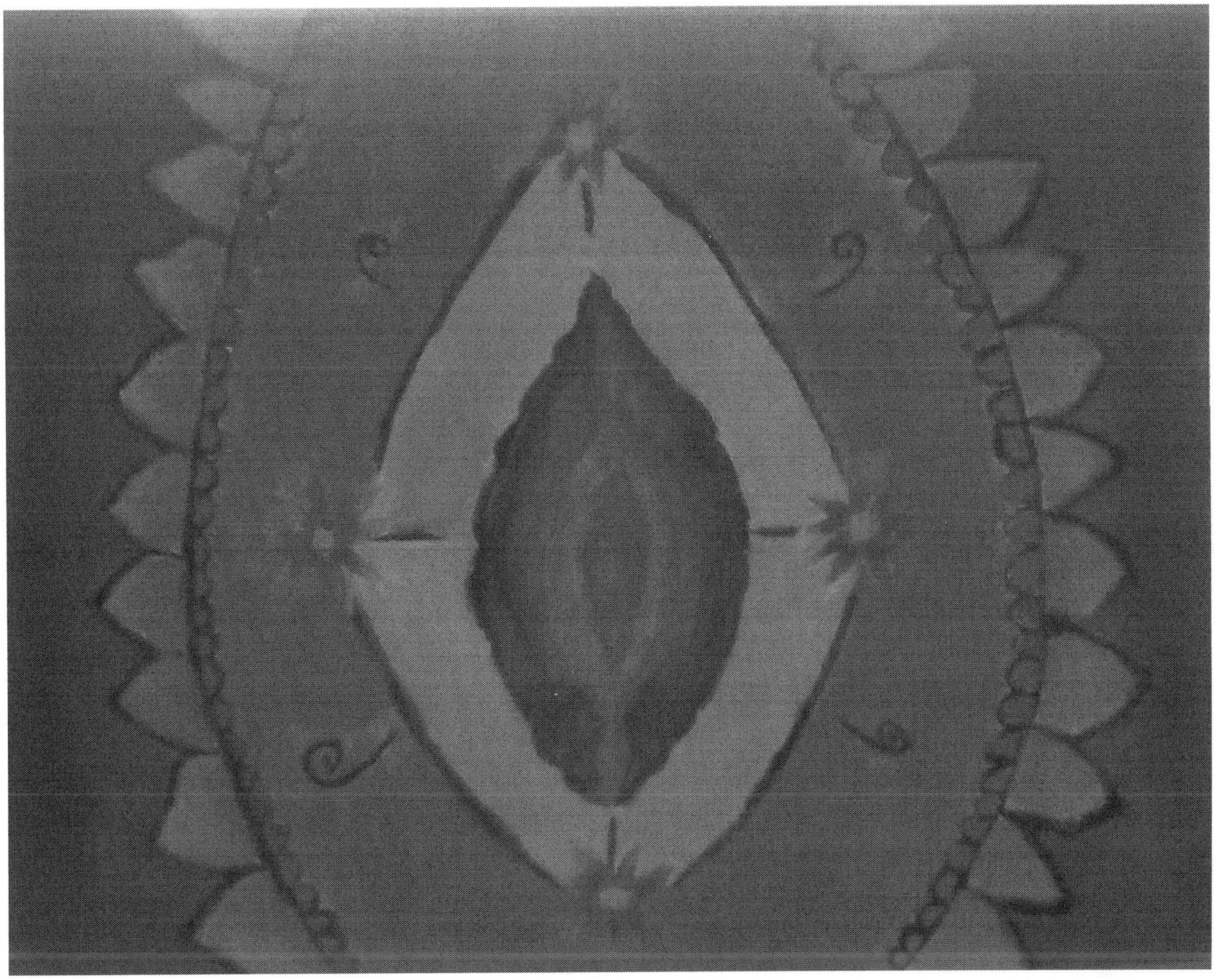

There is a path
the Goddess walks--
It's entered through
their soul.
And though I could
repeat it here,
They intuitively
Know.
It gives them inner confidence,
To know they live this way...
It is through their demeanor
That they glide through every day.

When the Goddess enters
The people want to see...
They wish to feel the power
of a soul that's truly free.
If you live as a Goddess,
Thank you for what you do.
And if you aren't there yet,
The best of luck to you.
The world needs peaceful people,
with spirit, fire, and soul;
To walk the Goddess path
Should be all humanity's goal.

Table of Contents

Materials Needed:

- Mirror, both large to stand in front of and hand held
- Pens, watercolors, markers, etc.
- Various herbs, oils, and spices (keep your favorites handy)
- Glass Jars and/or Clay
- Natural incense, resin, and herbs for burning
- A small bell, tambourine, drum or other instrument for clearing space and opening rituals. You may use your hands, voice and feet instead.
- Occasionally a bath, or natural waters such as a river or ocean.
- Patience
- Intuition
- Willingness
- Offerings to exchange with nature (pennies, seeds, liquor, spit, etc)

Dear Goddess,

Whatever your unique journey, the time has come to embrace yourself! Like the punani, none of us is born quite exactly the same, each with our own preferences, needs, and ways of expression, and with that it is an honor to walk on this Earth with one, though the burdens at times do seem numerous.

I have found time and again that those of us with punanis, wombs, womb spaces (I will sometimes call us "womb bearers" but try to avoid too many labels) tend to be filled with misinformation and depressing untruths about our own bodies! We are taught what we have is shameful and that being too inquisitive is useless and devilish and sluttish. With this workbook, I hope you will reach forth and find out just who you are, and how exciting that is. Invite one of the most powerful and inspiring parts of our physical body-- the womb! Reach deep and start making connections throughout your life to gain more answers...this workbook is only a beginning tool for a larger journey.

As more people reclaim the wise ancient ways and mix them with the innovative and sustainable modern ones, the future on Earth becomes a safer and more peaceful place to be. Your journey is for you, but it is also for your descendants and all of the lives you touch along the way.

Use this workbook however you like-- worked from front to back, perused through and used at leisure, or perhaps open at random and work in that way. Whatever you choose, allow this tool to work with you as you grow in your self-love and knowledge.

Peace on your path,

Tahtahme Nehandas Xero

The Sacred Bruja

thepathofagoddess@gmail.com

Honey Pot Chronicles: Prelude

Star Crossed Lovers

We
Never stood a chance.
Born
of time and place
I could not risk one touch or glance
for fear what others might think or do.
I tried to distract myself, but
impossible.
Even when I did not pay any mind,
someone else always did.
Something too strong to be restrained beneath the skirt,
the world always wondering what might be going on down there?
When I realized this power, I pawned it as currency
for my every need.
My punani stopped calling me.
I don't place blame.
I didn't care until
I felt that black hole stretch deep within me
And
Realized I could not pretend the power was not mine alone--
I--
swirling vortex of ether and
Love and
Melanin and Gold
I
Knew it was time.
I
poured libation and mourned.
I
praised my womb spirit.
I
called an inner name and then stood still
and though time passed,
the spirit came
and I
cried and
I
prayed and
We
embraced each other and
I
was invited home
Into the expanse of existence...

The Punani Proverbs

- Cherish your punani.
- Listen to your womb.
- Heed your yoni's needs.
- No womb is an island.
- A punani in need is a friend indeed.
- An empty womb will clutch at experiences.
- No other comes before your punani.
- No matter how gold the offering, the pussy is the power.
- A womb divided against its body cannot create.
- Every clitoris has its day.
- Knowledge feeds the punani.
- Feed the punani.
- Orgasm is an excellent form of defense.
- The punani is a temple. The soul decides the worship.
- A little of what the pussy fancies, does the soul good.

- A punani cannot change the curl of its hair.
- The punani is home.
- Every honey pot has a sweet spot.
- A wet pussy is as good as a dry one to a terrible lover.
- One punani is worth a thousand words.
- It's never the honey pot's fault.
- A punani shouldn't be a stranger on its own body.
- Punani is beauty-- Joy. Forever.
- A wet punani lifts all spirits.
- A voluntary punani is worth 1000 pressured ones.
- A watched punani never creams.
- Punani is only punani, but a person is an experience.
- Absolute power corrupts a punani.
- Better to enjoy the punani you have than to lust after one you don't.
- Your orgasm speaks louder than words.
- Better to orgasm once than to never orgasm at all.
- Horny pussy always risks it.
- The wise womb expects the unexpected.
- A womb is never finished creating.
- Publicity is good for the punani-- shame is death.
- Fuck no punani, hear no lies.
- All the world loves a punani that glistens.
- Where you grow your hairs, so must you decorate with flowers.
- Punani to womb, emotion to reaction, physical to spiritual.
- There is no bad punani-- only bad intellect.
- Be careful what you manifest-- the womb remembers.
- Better to enjoy the punani than to curse its burn.
- Blessed is the punani.
- Pleasure and the punani are equals.
- Clean punani is a Goddess Thing.
- Punanis find comparisons odious.
- The punani always pays.
- Happy pussy, warm heart.

- All vaginas are desired from a distance.
- Do unto your punani what it does unto you.
- Don't confuse yoni pleasure with yoni business.
- Don't put old news onto new punani.
- The way to a punani is through the soul.

The Punani Proverbs:
Extended Study

****Use the frames at the back of the book to make small cards of these and your own Punani Proverbs.***

- **Cherish your punani.**
  Love your womb, vulva, and body unapologetically. Treat yourself with the utmost love and care. Enjoy your divinity. Protect your body and protect the sacred esteem in which you hold yourself. Do not let anyone move you from this good opinion you have of yourself. If you should falter in maintaining this good standing, do better starting now. Every tiny nuance and unique detail about you should be cherished, even as you grow and change with each week and year.
  Notes:

- **Listen to your womb.**
  Nothing should ever *really* sneak up on you...your womb is always

talking, always sending out messages to you-- and it is your job to listen. Sometimes these chats you both will have are physical (in the form of pain or pleasure) and sometimes they are spiritual (in the form of a gut instinct or new experience). At times these messages will come so fast that you barely realize they have arrived before they are gone...other times it will feel like you and your womb are pulling all-nighters trying to talk it out. Respect each of these interactions and take the time to truly listen to what you are being told both literally and symbolically.*Notes:*

- **Heed your yoni's needs.**
  Never assume that your needs are going to be the same as someone else's, even a little bit. Sometimes they are, and that is a fun surprise of synchronicity, but many times your needs are very different, and this is normal! You can always enjoy someone else's journey while respecting that what they are doing is not your path. Remember to follow through with yourself...listen closely to your needs, take notes of your likes and dislikes, and pamper yourself every once in a while in the special ways that you personally enjoy.
  Notes:

- **No womb is an island.**
Millions of people had to meet, love, take a chance, hate, argue, live, die and grow to reach the point where you stand before us today. The DNA within your cells is testament to the lives that came before you...your Ancestors. You were born of the collective…Every choice you make does ultimately affect those around you, not just today, but in the generations to come. To thrive in wellness, you must respect that you (and all of us) are connected through time.
Notes:

- **A punani in need is a friend indeed.**
Respecting your punanis wants and needs goes far beyond acknowledging them or figuring out your own preferences. Do you listen when your very *destiny* calls your name? When your true inner calling speaks to your soul, do you follow this inner voice of power, or do you allow other people outside of you to dictate where your life goes instead?
Notes:

- **An empty womb will clutch at experiences.**
  When the womb goes through periods of spiritual emptiness (depression, grief, and trauma), the natural response is to try and refill it. These emotions are not avoidable, nor should you be trying to avoid them. Rather, you should rely on the healing methods, healers, teachers, tools, and spiritual connections you have been building during times of wellness, as well as the power that is naturally coursing through your blood.
  Notes:

- **No other comes before your punani.**
  This goes for any genitals of anybody else on this planet! Cherish what you have and do not neglect and overlook your needs-- even for family. Take the time you need to listen to yourself, care for yourself, or even (Yes!) pamper yourself on a regular basis. Take care of yourself, live by example, and you will inspire the world.
  Notes:

- **No matter how gold the offering, the pussy is the power.**
  It doesn't matter what anyone else is offering-- if they are trying to exchange or give anything, it is because you have power. Do not be afraid of your power and do not underestimate it. Within your sacred seat is a vortex of potent energy...this is yours and it is precious. When you believe someone else is in control of this energy, they can begin to use your energy and manipulate it for their own desires. Don't let others convince you the trick lies in super expensive remedies, or completely in gurus and one particular method. You have power and beauty in yourself that can nurture and create and *needs* to in addition to outside sources.
  Notes:

- **A womb divided against its body cannot create.**
  When you acknowledge that your womb holds power and potential beyond the limits of your imagination, you only scratch at all of the layers of possibility this information gives you. The womb has certain needs and requirements-- some are beyond your control, but others are not, and many others still can be simulated by you for your health and healing. If you choose not to listen to your own womb's spiritual and physical needs, you choose to invite whatever consequences arrive.
  Notes:

- **Every clitoris has its day.**
  That day is sometimes awarded in a ceremonial manner, and sometimes that day is unexpected, spontaneous, and delightfully refreshing. The true question is, will you know your day when it is happening? Will you appreciate what your day is? Can you release all expectations for your day to be the same as or measure similarly to someone else's?
  Notes:

- **Knowledge feeds the punani.**
  Certain knowledge always remains constant. That you are backed by your Ancestors and that there is within you immense power and potential are some to start. But within you is the ever abiding need to always go further, and you must always remember to stay open to being a humble student.
  Notes:

- **Feed the punani.**
  Set aside the time for yourself. Pamper yourself. You know what you should be doing, so why do you not do it? Put in the time and you will get the results that you have been craving. When you feel that things in your life are stagnant or slow, jumpstart your womb's creative juices with something healing that will move you on the right track.
  Notes:

- **Orgasm is an excellent form of defense.**
  Your climax has the power to heal, create, defend, manifest, attack, relax and rejuvenate. It is one of the most powerful personal tools that you have in your arsenal. Never forget to use it to give yourself the advantage. Use discernment to decide what form of energy you need your orgasmic energy to take. Decide what your plan is before you start and utilize your pleasure for your advancement spiritually, physically and socially. Do not feel like it has to be screaming, wild, or traditional. Try something new. Be you.
  Notes:

- **The punani is a temple. The soul decides the worship.**
  Your body is *your* temple. You are the Priestess of this area, and it is up to you to truly decide what is going to happen here. What is respect to *you*? What matters to you? Where do you draw the line? What are things that you were raised to think are terrible but don't feel are that bad? Again, this is your temple. You make up the rules because that is your divine right.
  Notes:

- **A little of what the pussy fancies, does the soul good.**
  Indulge. There are ways to do this that can help you grow...and ways to do this that will wreck your entire life. The key is figuring out which is which for you. What are you here for in life? One answer should always be to feed your soul.
  Notes:

- **A punani cannot change the curl of its hair.**
  No matter what some might say, no one will ever have quite your look, smell, touch, or feel. No other punani will have your flavor. No other womb has quite your quirks and needs. Rather than this being a subject of shame or embarrassment, allow this to fuel you. Allow it to press you forward. The fact that no one else has just this combination allows you to create in ways that no one else really can. Cherish this.
  Notes:

- **The punani is home.**
  Feel good with your pussy. When your body talks to you throughout the day, even just conversationally...listen. Answer back. You might just hear something that you both need to know, something you might actually love or need, and you don't have to respond out loud, but you can respond! Remind your punani you are thinking of your mutual wellness. Allow your conversations to be secretive, as with a friend; reach out and remind your punani that you're in this together.
  Notes:

- **Every honey pot has a sweet spot.**
  A sweet spot is when the ultimate combination comes together to optimally connect and culminate into perfection. Your life is full of them. Through your spiritual work you can manifest them. Though you sometimes might feel like this moment isn't coming, it is. It is your birthright to experience them.
  Notes:

- **A wet pussy is as good as a dry one to a terrible lover.**
  Some people, places, situations, and things, don't give a damn about you. They just don't. Let them go from your mind, from your heart, from your soul. Cut the cords that connect them from your womb space to their own Sacred Seat. Release them from yourself periodically to give your life what it truly needs.
  Notes:

- **One punani is worth a thousand words.**
  Your punani and your womb are complex both physically and energetically. All is connected to who we are, what we have been through, and what we want to be. Do not fear or doubt the effectiveness of your personal power.
  Notes:

- **It's never the honey pot's fault.**
  Even if your honey pot leaks honey everywhere, there are signs the day was coming. Part of becoming more intimate with your womb is knowing its wants and needs, as well as which tools and rituals work best for you. It's having the intuition to know when to spend time with yourself and on yourself. This takes time and patience and is not a skill learned overnight.
  Notes:

- **A punani shouldn't be a stranger on its own body.**
  Embrace the needs that birth real slow from your sacred core. When you indulge in and follow them correctly, they shape you and help you grow. Even needs you do not wish to use or indulge in still need acknowledgement and release. When you ignore those needs because of internal or external hangups, you invite excess trauma and mishaps into your own life.
  Notes:

- **Your punani is a beauty. Joy. Forever.**
  Appreciate the special dimples and curves, appreciate the smells-- all of them. Come to learn what they mean. The energy pulsing within you is never ending and never disappearing. It is the energy of your Ancestors, cycling over and over, to be cherished as it uplifts. Consider yourself as great and beautiful as the Taj Mahal, the greatest romance poem, or any other great work of art.
  Notes:

- **A wet punani lifts all spirits.**
  When your needs are met, the rivers of abundance can flow-- when the circumstances aren't set up correctly, it should be expected that this will not be. Work on facilitating those circumstances that can lead to ultimate pleasure, release, and energetic flow.
  Notes:

- **A voluntary punani is worth 1000 pressured ones.**
  To unleash the power of your Sacred Seat, you must work with your own personal needs. It does not matter what others are doing with theirs, what are you doing with yours? Is it what your body truly wants or needs, or is it what others around you are saying that you want and need? Do not feel pressured to conform to any norms...instead take the time to determine what your personal norms are.
  When a Womb is worked with in alignment to its needs (versus outside

needs projecting onto it for their own sake) true magic can happen. When a Womb is expected to act like someone else's in perfection... it often falters. Find your own strengths and abilities so that you can use your power accordingly.
Notes:

- **A watched punani never creams.**
If your plan is to sit and wait for things to happen how you dream, you are going to start feeling like nothing ever happens to you, sooner or later. Take the "down time" while you are trying to facilitate the right circumstances and fill it with the abundance you seek! Conjure up some of your greatest needs-- confidence, intelligence, discipline, and more...
Notes:

- **Punani is only punani, but a person is an experience.**
Everyone who has a pussy has a nice one. There is nothing about yours that is more (or less) special than anyone else's. You are not your vagina; you are you and you happen to have a punani that you connect with on an intimate level. This is all well and dandy, but you are a person, not a punani! Your punani cannot do all the work for you and never expect it to. Assuming your vagina is better than someone else's

just because it's yours is a fatal flaw. Your answers can be better found elsewhere.

Notes:

- **Absolute power corrupts a punani.**

  Of course you should have absolute power over your own punani, but your punani should *never* have absolute power over *you*. Following your every hormonal and womb-driven need leads to a corruption not only over your relationship with your pussy energy, but also with your overall goals that reach far beyond your needs within the root aritu. Balance is key to your vitality.

  Notes:

- **Better to enjoy the punani you have, than to lust after one you don't.**

  As the lovely Leah Smith once sang, "I am beautifully and wonderfully made!" Just like fingerprints, no two punanis are the same! None smell the same; none have exactly the same labia; none are the same inside. The one you have is special, and only you were gifted with it. Forget any industry or simple pink drawings that make you feel inadequate or so different you should feel ashamed. You are so different you should

feel *exalted.* The craftsmanship behind your punani is literally one of a kind, passed through the bloodline and spirit. Celebrate that.
Notes:

- **Your orgasm speaks louder than words.**
  Do you spend time talking about what it is you are going to do, but never actually get around to reaching the peak? Leave that habit behind, please. No. Seriously. You talking big game about taking control of your sensuality, sexuality, goals, and life in general is all well and dandy...but how many times have you actually screamed or had your breath caught up in your throat??? Sometimes it is time to just *take action* and push until you finish.
  Notes:

- **Better to orgasm once than to never orgasm at all.**
  Are you holding yourself back from life's ultimate pleasures? Why? Who or what obligation is more important than you are? When you see the word "once" be reminded that *yes*. You are worth it at least *one* time, *right*? What about two? What about three? Your life is yours, be sure to cherish yourself and your own needs while you are living it!
  Notes:

- **Horny pussy always risks it.**
  Horny, desperate, virile pussy energy is some strong stuff, and damn hard to control. We have all been there. And we all know that if you let it get too far, it will start to have you doing things you *never* saw yourself doing before. It doesn't matter if there have been witnesses to you being overcome or not, the fact remains that if you do not keep your energy in check it can rule you. Don't stop with charting your moods during your cycle...do something with that energy before it does something with you.
  Notes:

- **The wise womb expects the unexpected.**
  In the ideal world, the village and community would always be by your side. In the modern world, however, most of us experience life much differently. It is better to be ready than be unprepared, always. Therefore, expect that you will be the only one with your goals and dreams at the forefront of their mind. Expect that others will forget, and only you will remember. And if you let the world do something for

you, prepare yourself for what to do when others do not follow through.
Notes:

- **A womb is never finished creating.**
Whether you are disconnected from your womb spiritually, you had nine babies in your womb or none at all, it was physically removed in whole or in part, or you never had one, none of this matters. The energy within your root aritu is a creative one--the perfect space for incubating eggs as well as ideas, plans, and much more. So long as your soul continues this journey, your days of creation are not over!
Notes:

- **Publicity is good for the punani-- shame is death.**
Empower other punanis, don't mortify them. Encourage other punanis, don't envy them. Normalize the functions associated with the pussy and womb, don't hide them. Knowledge is the best way to make having one and using it for your own wants and needs acceptably...let the facts be your friend. Through your life, language and reactions, you can show others daily just how much respect the vaginas (and those who are attached to them) deserve, no matter what they are doing!
Notes:

- **Fuck no punani, hear no lies.**
  If you take no chances, you won't ever get burned. That doesn't mean you should live your life in fear of what might happen next, however. That means all choices have risks, all choices have consequences (positive and negative) and there is no avoiding this. So why do we try to avoid this if it is everyday life?
  Furthermore, there are always going to be people who do not tell you the truth, whether you think it reasonable or not. If you stay at home all day and never talk to a soul, you will never hear these lies. Just saying.
  Notes:

- **All the world loves a punani that glistens.**
  It is easy to get support when you are at your best or in alignment with what makes the world most comfortable. It is a little harder when who you are makes the world uncomfortable…You begin to run into roadblocks and those who are angry that you seem more free or happy than they did when they were in your place. This is not your problem. Even when the world is in alignment with your needs, this isn't your

problem. The world is full of wishy washy people--stick with what *you* want and just go with that.

Notes:

- **Where you grow your hairs, so must you decorate with flowers.** Cherish how your body *is*. Celebrate the subtle nuances and love the little secret parts that no one will ever know. Treat your pussy with reverence, treat your punani as an altar. Decorate, praise, meditate with, and enjoy. Inaugurate your glory with a crown of flowers.

  Notes:

- **Punani to womb, emotion to reaction, physical to spiritual.** Do not make the mistake of spending so much time on one particular idea or skill. Each small part makes up the whole. Remaining wholistic is the key, especially when making decisions that keep you balanced between what you are living now and what goes on Beyond.

  Notes:

- **There is no bad punani-- only bad intellect.**
  There is no pussy on Earth that is actually better than another. Don't get in your head about what you should or shouldn't look like or be able to do! Instead, embrace fully your own wants, needs, and goals, and walk towards them without any worries of what those still caught up in "the rules" may be thinking.
  Notes:

- **Be careful what you manifest-- the womb remembers.**
  You are constantly manifesting, whether you realize it or not. As they say, "Having is evidence of wanting." You are already a swirling vortex of energy, intentions, and power...it is *well* worth your while to take the time to learn to control your own mind and thoughts! If you are in the habit of letting your mind run free consistently, be patient with yourself as you work to undo these impulses.
  Notes:

- **Better to enjoy the punani than to curse its burn.**
  Enjoy your passions. Enjoy your impulses. Enjoy the things that cause you to feel, grow, and *be*. Of course, life has no set path, but you are special and unique and only *you* burn quite the way that you do! Respect and enjoy this and follow the instinctual spirit that rears its head within you.
  Notes:

- **Blessed is the punani.**
  At times it can seem like a curse, but your body and you are both equally a blessing. You don't have to be an expert on your punani, or anyone else's, to love and cherish what you have. The blessings that flow forth from the vast eclectic energies around your womb are unstoppable-- a waterfall of abundant glory from your very bloodline.
  Notes:

- **Pleasure and the punani are equals.**
  There is no need to punish your pussy or to deny either of you of pleasure. Your punani has done nothing wrong and not only enjoys and gives pleasure, but thrives through creative manifestation under careful care. This doesn't mean that your every whim should be followed, only that with use of this beautiful energy you can go much further with embracing instead of rejection. Your pleasure is always *yours* first and foremost.
  Notes:

- **Clean punani is a Goddess Thing.**
  Your pussy is a naturally self-cleaning organ. That doesn't mean that you don't have to put effort into helping out! Today's world is full of toxins that are chemical, physical, spiritual, familial, national, and more... With these stressful poisons around every step you make it is important to put in the time and effort to really consider what you are using on and in your body. Keeping your colon clean helps the womb float freely. And keeping your womb free of stress and other energies facilitates your own personal healing. Indulgence is all well and dandy, but when you are looking for real results, *work* and *effort* are needed!
  Notes:

- **Punanis find comparisons odious.**
  When two punanis are compared, a disservice is done to both. Knowing how futile it is to really compare parts so unique and personal, what then is the point? Do not shame others, and most of all, don't deem to insult yourself with comparisons. Your womb does not like it, and neither should you.
  Notes:

- **The punani always pays.**
  What goes up, must come down. What goes in, must come out. What is created will be birthed, though perhaps not in the way that you assume. Consequences (both positive and negative) are to be expected with every choice that is made.
  Notes:

- **Happy pussy, warm heart.**
  When you are happy, doesn't the world usually seem happy too? The same law applies here...when you care for yourself and take the time to indulge yourself and keep yourself happy, you spread this energy into your entire life.
  Notes:

- **All vaginas are desired from a distance.**
  Many lust after what they can't have. Remember that this is *never* to be mistaken for love or actual affection under any circumstances. Plenty of people will want what they can't have, or what seems like (to them) an easy *or* hard "catch" to sexually manipulate or assault you. Sexual acts do not.
  Notes:

- **Do unto your punani what you want done to you.**
  Your body is there for you. It's more loyal than pretty much anyone else that you know. Before others were there, your punani was there. Even when it starts to fail you, know that it is doing it's best with what it has. Respect friendship like that with your own kind habits. Do the little things that all add up together to create a beautiful relationship.
  Notes:

- **Don't confuse yoni pleasure with yoni business.**
  Just because you like it, doesn't mean it is best for you. Just because you enjoy it, does not make it good for you. And conversely, sometimes the things that you have no interest in at all, or really would rather avoid are actually what might be best for you! Follow your intuition as well as your inner wisdom and knowledge.
  Notes:

- **Don't put old news onto new punani.**
  When you grow, you evolve. Don't go back. Leave the old habits in the past. It is okay to totally leave your old news behind and never return to them as a lifestyle again.
  Notes:

- **The way to a punani is through the soul.**
  No, this is not about how your lovers should fall in love with you. It's about how *you* should get to know *yourself.* Treat yourself...Wine and dine yourself. Get to know yourself intimately. You are an amazing person who deserves not only romance but also pleasure...and a true friend who cares. Care for yourself, your power, and your womb--individually as well as a unit.
  Notes:

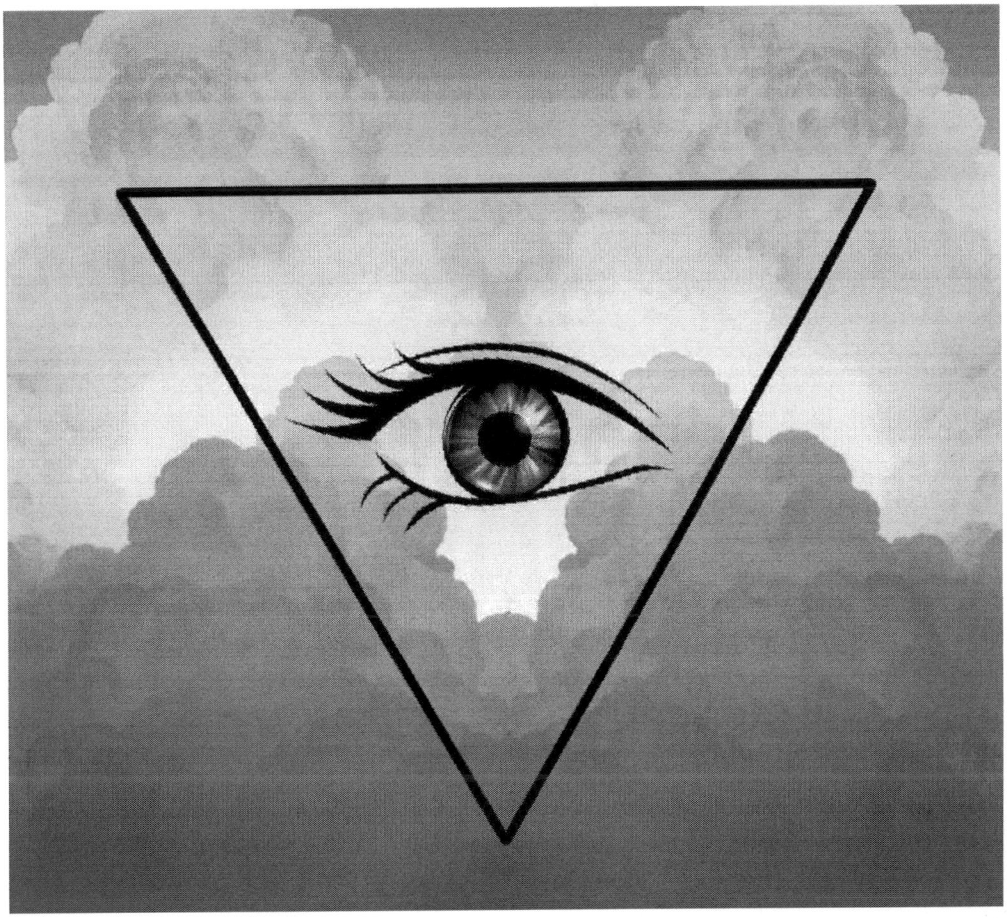

Part One: An Introduction

Honey Pot Chronicles #1

Let sun caress vulva
Spread oil across each inch of skin
Let it melt between the folds and slide...
With patience, come to know
each sacred sense
of feeling that you have--
Learn to melt at your own hand.
Learn how to keep a secret,
safe between the two of you.
Give a fond hello,
Don't be a stranger in your skin.

There is power in understanding and knowledge...especially in the energy that naturally courses through your own body. There is a power within the womb--this power can be masculine, feminine, a mix of both, or not quite either one. This workbook focuses on the feminine, however there is endless potential in all directions.

Only *your* vessel holds all the strange nuanced differences that create the person *you* are. Each individual string comes together, winding into a web creating the individual. Who chose your body? What powers lay in this womb and why? Only you can answer these question through serious self-reflection and meditation, as well as spiritual readings from initiated and trained leaders and elders that you trust..

Energy throughout our body carries so much potential, but the Womb Energy is intriguing and vast. It allows you the opportunity to, when you come to know your womb, come to love yourself and thusly appreciate the entire package of your body exactly as it was given.

You are not your body--you are your soul yet, in this experience, at this time, it all seems to meld into one creation called "yourself." It is vitally important to understand the true power of the body you were given in the essence of what it is and what you can do...it is important to love the body you were given and understand the true power this body has, and why you were meant to wield this power.

Norms at this time in your healing journey are frivolous. **Don't fear your unique qualities. Don't be controlled by your enemies' fear.** Likewise, while you come to understand your own limitations, don't hesitate to continue to love yourself!

For the Introduction section, we will get to know you as an individual, you as the collective, you as a body, and you as a dream for the future. When you write it all down it gives you an opportunity to interview and come to understand yourself in an intimate manner that few take the time to really do (tragically).

As you delve deeper you may come to reveal and recognize facets of your inner self that you have never noticed before...you may also come to realize that old held beliefs conflict with new ones, or that new practices negate old ones...this is all normal as you grow and learn to keep your womb in a constant state of abundance and health.

You will learn as you practice remaining in this centered space what it is that suits you and what it is that you needed to let go of for your own personal well being. Cherish each of these nuances, even when they leave you lonely or misunderstood. Each of them ties in to the you that is at the core of all of this being.

What is your full name? If you have a name that isn't your born name, use the one that you prefer.

Draw a picture of your face:

Draw a picture of the top of your head:

Draw a picture of your chest:

Draw a picture of your stomach:

Draw a picture of your booty in your favorite clothes:

Draw your soul:

Draw your third eye:

Draw yourself doing yoga:

Draw your smile:

Draw yourself with your womb opening up as a portal:

What is your height? Draw yourself with height proportionate surroundings:

What is your weight? What is your ideal weight? Draw both pictures:

Year You Were Born:

Hair Length:

Use 10 words to describe yourself:

What is the nickname you have given yourself? (If you don't have any, explain why.)

Have you nicknamed any parts of your body? (If you don't have any, explain why.)

Which 4 fictional characters are you the most like? How do you relate to them?

Which 4 fictional characters do you wish you were like? Why do you admire them?

What is your favorite childhood memory? Why?

Do you use your head or your heart more?

What is your outlet when you are angry?

What do you do when you are sad?

How do you mourn?

Who do you go to when you are upset?

When are you the most vulnerable?

Are you brave?

Are you more afraid of dying, or are you more afraid of not living your fullest life? Why?

Are you more afraid of being forgotten by history, or are you more afraid of not having anyone to enjoy you while you are here?

Do you believe in life partners, soul mates, kindred spirits, or similar spiritual partnerships between two humans, either sexual or not? What is the difference among them? Have you ever experienced any of these? Who with?

To you, God/a higher power is:

What does it take to earn your trust?

What does it take to get to have sex with you?

Use 5 words to describe how you believe other people see you:

Use 5 words to describe how you would like for people to see you:

If you had to choose family or friends, who would you choose? Why?

What are you most grateful for about your life? Why?

What do you wish you could change about your life? Why?

What/Who are you willing to sacrifice for your womb wellness?

What/Who are you willing to sacrifice for your spiritual wellness?

What/Who are you willing to sacrifice to gain a healthy relationship with your Ancestors?

What is manifestation to you?

Have you ever manifested before? If so, who taught you how to manifest?

In your wildest imagination, what could you manifest?

Who is the most powerful manifestor/practitioner that you know? What makes them powerful? Do you see any of these qualities in yourself? Is this the best way to be powerful (in your opinion)?

What would you like to manifest in the next year?

What would you like to manifest in the next five years?

What would you like to manifest in the next ten years?

What would you like to manifest before you die?

If you could choose one person in the world to manifest with on an energetic (not necessarily sexual) level for the rest of your existence as a soul, who would that person be and why?

What was the greatest moment of impact on you in your entire life? How did it shape you? Who else was involved in this moment?

When was the first time you remember learning about your womb?

What was the first time you did something spiritual with your womb?

If you had to give your womb a name, what would you choose?

Does your womb menstruate (bleed) regularly?

Explain what happens when the womb menstruates? (In general).

What type of relationship did you have with your parents?

What type of relationship do you have (OR do you want to have) with your children? Answer about youth in general if you do not plan to have children.

Describe your first period, what happened, who you told, and how it was handled.

What should happen for a youth when their womb begins menstruating for the first time? (feel free to draw pictures, write poetry, write a script, etc.)

How do you think your parents (and other adults in your life) let you down when it came to womb knowledge and womb health?

Who do you talk to when you have a question about your womb or womb health?

Who do you think young womb bearers should talk to about their reproductive health?

Why is it important to teach people in general about womb health?

How do you show your passion and belief about womb health in your everyday life and activity?

What do you do to celebrate your womb space?

Draw a picture of your punani:

When was the first time you really *looked* at your punani?

What is your vulva's best feature? Why do you like this one?

What is your vulva's worst feature? Why do you think this?

What would you change about the outward appearance of your vagina if you could? Why? What would happen to/for you if this change occurred?

Stand in front of a mirror. Undress slowly, taking the utmost care with each movement. Don't take your eyes off your body as though you are a desperate lover of yours who has not seen your body in half a millenia, but is now afforded one final glimpse before an eternity of solitude. Draw the nude your lover would have drawn to keep and cherish forever. Be as abstract or concrete in your depiction as you desire.

Return to the mindset of the lover from the previous prompt. Staring upon your naked body after undressing with care and purpose...write yourself a love letter or poem...an ode to the flesh and glory that relaxes before you. Do not flex or suck in anything. Enjoy every sensual inch.

Imagine the most erotic night that you would love to participate in. Confess...what is it? Who is there? What happens to you? Where does it take place? Why are you so comfortable?

Draw your womb using nothing but stars, planets & objects from space:

Do you ever look at the outside of your punani? What do you think of your vulva? Why?

Draw yourself as Venus in the Birth of Venus--using your own image as your muse. Feel free to create an entirely personal interpretation of the Birth. Be as symbolic and wild as you feel necessary.

Draw yourself as an Air Goddess or Spirit.

Draw yourself as a Fire Goddess or Spirit.

Draw yourself as a Water Goddess or Spirit.

Draw yourself as Asase Yaa (Mother Earth).

Draw yourself as an Ancestor.

Write an advertisement for your own pussy. Make it as appealing as possible. Be sure to include a visual, as pictures say a thousand words!

7 Monday Challenge

The modern Monday has become a day most people despise, but it might motivate you to know that it is the day of the Ancestors! It is a wonderful day to embrace beginnings, change the water on your altar, give your Ancestors some drinks and treats, wash the floor, be grateful for what you have and focus on your spiritual healing and needs for the week.

Every Monday for the next seven Mondays, let's make a commitment to spend time getting to know your womb (and Ancestors) in fun and relaxing ways. We will learn the parts, meditate on them, and come to truly enjoy our womb over this seven session process. But don't let yourself slap the workbook closed and be done! Follow each prompt carefully and focus on each symbol mentioned in each chapter to really allow yourself to connect with your womb the way that every person who is near a womb on a daily basis should do.

When you are done with each challenge, allow your curiosity to pull you farther into study and knowledge. Don't be satisfied with how *I* say things work or are--go try and see for yourself! Books, workbooks, and classes are only your foundation; it is in the real-life application and personal reflection that you will begin to understand how *you* manipulate and utilize energy in particular.

Remember that many of the traditions of Hoodoo are passed through the bloodline, but for a lot of people this information has been lost through the years and generations. **If you do not do the trial and error to find what works for you and yours again, who will?** What works for someone else may not work for you, so do not be discouraged if you find yourself tweaking wording, offerings or other details to what you find described or spoken to you.

1st Monday -
Self-Love Jar

<u>Prayer to Your Ancestors</u>: *I call to the Ancestors both known and unknown. Knowing your love is powerful and inspiring in my life....you love and look out for me, even when I hate and sabotage myself. Thank you for my body, my breath, my soul, and my future. Please, teach me Self-Love. Help me to radiate with the love and excellence of those who came before me, and continue their proud tradition. Allow my every action and reaction to be rooted in my self-wellness and love. Increase my Self-Love until my entire mind, spirituality, and life is transformed greater than I ever dreamed. Whatever my goals are, let them be accomplished through my powerful self-love.*

Beginning with a Self-Love jar gives you something to visually keep an eye on for the next few months as you complete this workbook. It allows you to focus first and foremost on yourself and what negative or positive things you think of your body, cast them away, and choose instead to embrace all flaws and skills and everything that they do (and don't) have to offer.

Even if you have amazing self-esteem, you should still consider working your roots with this jar. Focusing on your positive self-image allows you to improve your confidence as well as nip your negative thoughts in the bud before they blossom out of control. Pampering yourself even, for the good it has done in the past is vital for continued kindness towards yourself in the future.

A special way to do this is to create a love sweet jar for yourself. Working Jars have long been a staple in Hoodoo, but have grown to be adopted by other American Folk magic as the popularity of this simple method has spread.

Use of a jar for magic can be traced back to what is today called the Congo. Most people who look into these specific vessel rituals, commonly attribute the African American practices of Face Jugs and use of jars and oil lamps as containers, to have originated from the Nkisi dolls found throughout the Congo Basin and Central Africa. Where the hollow belly of the dolls were kept hollow to be filled with herbs and small items, then plugged to close, African people made or purchased a jug with only the face to represent the spirit or used a simple jar and lid. Face Jugs were also used by Black Americans to guard homes and graves, as well as spirits on their way to the spirit world. Considering not only these, but various West African tribes (which never really succumbed to Islam the way other parts of Africa did) arrived on the coasts from Louisiana to North Carolina, we can see how continuation of African Traditional Religion and its practices were abundant among African Americans.

Jar magic can be positive or negative--it all depends on the energy and prayer that you put into it. Above all else it is important to remember to keep working at what you have started; Rootwork is definitely *not* a "set it and forget it" activity! When you see my recipes (or other ones online and in books) remember to use them for inspiration only. Look for ingredients that stand out to you. Do not overspend through some major corporation--this is not the way to make your magic work. Again, the time and energy you spend on your work is more important, as is being particular about your ingredient choice for *personal* reason. If the Work is serious, consider including DNA (spit, hair, blood, etc). If the work is *very* serious, consider hiring a professional.

When you finish making your jar and set it on your altar, come back to it all the time. Come back again and again, and consider your progress in your goal. Check in with yourself. Carry the jar outside every month on the full moon. Smoke a blunt with it. Work on it.

<u>You Will Need:</u>

- A glass jar with a lid. You can also make a clay jar* and cover the opening later.
- One pretty card OR a piece of paper you have decorated.
- A lock of your own hair.
- Essential oils (chamomile, lavender, geranium, rose, bergamot, frankincense, white fir, myrrh, mint, orange), and/or fresh or dried herbs (pink sea salt, jasmine petals, chamomile, lemon balm, rose (buds, powder or petals), lavender, aloe, beet juice, etc)
- Two different colored pens/writing utensils
- 1 full and blooming flower, with a stem, gathered from somewhere in your neighborhood
- Flowers, petals, and leaves also gathered during your walk through the neighborhood
- Simple Syrup**
- 21 tea lights / candles. Substitute all but 1 with crystals, shells or other sacred items as necessary.

<u>*Making a Face Jug:</u>

Face Jugs, often called Ugly Jugs by our Ancestors, are sadly today only made by *one* African American traditional potter who learned from his elders. Jim "The Black Potter" McDowell alone has been able to pass along the oral tradition to the next generation, using the same throwing and firing techniques used by Southern Ancestors over a century ago. He reminds us of the sacred practice of using face jugs as grave markers, with faces scary enough to get the Devil and Demons of America away from the soul, allowing it to rise to paradise without trauma. He, as well as other rootworkers, conjure people, and witch-doctors, also mention the act of infusing spirit and power into them, using them for personal belongings, rootwork, and as protectors of the home (sitting in the front or back).

It is not uncommon for non-Black people in the United States, most often White, to spend their resources excavating these centuries old grave markers in the South, and sell them as relics of times passed to private investors. Many times, when people see traditional Face Jugs today, they are sadly on sale for 10s and sometimes 100s of thousands of dollars at auctions online, and it's clear the intentions of all of this is to ignore the African American community who these objects rightfully belong to, while making money and denying dignity to the Ancestors. It is also not uncommon to see most Face Jugs of modern day created without any of the spiritual components by the descendants of White people in the Southern Appalachian mountains. Their Ancestors picked up the practice from local Black folk, not truly understanding what it was, but enjoying the aesthetic or general usefulness.

<u>Tools for Making the Jug:</u>

- Water
- Clay (from a river nearby, or my preference terracotta which is earthy yet air dries. Feel free to experiment with any clay you prefer and make your jugs truly modern and your own)
- "Slip" (aka clay mixed with water to make a sort of glue to hold clay parts together)
- Clay shaping tools (toothpick, chopstick, knife, rolling pin, molds)
- Decorations (beads, charms, shells, acrylic/watercolor paints)
- Clay surface coat spray
- A whole lot of Ashe.

Instructions:

**Note: be sure to breath prayer and song into your every motion of this practice.*

- Set the mood - Go somewhere peaceful, turn on music that is relevant, smoke cleanse, pray, call the Ancestors, etc.
- Take your water and pour it into a bowl. Mix it with a cinnamon stick and bless it with your sacred words.
- Portion out two pieces of clay and roll them into two palm sized balls. As you roll them, breath on each piece.
- Taking one clay ball, stick your thumb in the center and begin pinching around the outside with your other fingers, making a bowl with your pinching motion (what is commonly called in clay making a "pinch pot"). Stick your other thumb in and use your fingers to turn the ball around as you shape it into a bowl. This ancient bowl making method has been used across cultures and time to create simple, yet beautiful pottery.
- Do the same to the other ball so that you have two small bowls that are the same size around the rim.
- Using your tools, make small lines/marks on the rims of your two bowls. These help the two parts glue together, so they are less likely to break apart later.
- Apply slip to the rims of your two bowls, but don't rub out the marks.
- Put the two sides together and gently begin connecting the two sides by smearing the clay on both over the open part. Continue until it is smooth and both sides are connected like a ball, hollow inside and smooth on the outside.
- Choose which side will be the bottom and place it down on the ground to flatten it. With your tools, make a hole at the top of your jug and slowly widen it with a circular motion.
- Using extra clay, begin created eyes, nose and mouth. Attach them by making small marks on the back and applying slip, then slowly smoothing the connection with your hands and tools until seamless.

- Apply your beads, charms, shells and other items that will need to be pushed into soft clay.
- Allow the jar to begin drying, out of direct sunlight. Keep an eye on it! Mend any cracks you begin to notice as time goes on. You can keep this jar how it is, but remember that it will be temporary only this way. Applying a coating will help avoid it breaking, disintegrating, or losing the distinction of features.
- (At this time you can choose to pray and anoint your jar in an oil you have blessed or infused, or purchased from a trusted source. You can choose to smoke cleanse it as well).
- When the jar is mostly or completely dry, apply paint. You can paint while the clay is wet, however the effect will be a little more rough.
- When you are finished with your jug, allow it to dry outside and apply a coat of surface spray to protect your jug. Do this 2-3 times, according to instructions on the can.
- Put aside a little clay with which to plug your jug up after filling it with the chosen ingredients.

For a visual reference of how to make your own face jug, please view the YouTube video: “Sacred Sister Circle #30 Hoodoo Face Jugs Handmade Oil Lamp” (youtube.com/watch?v=Pu2gf6D_lok)

Notes/Sketches:

__Simple Syrup:__**

You can research and make your own personal recipes for your sweetening jar, but **the base of the syrup recipe is always equal parts cane sugar and water mixed together** and melted down on low over heat for a few minutes (unless you are seriously pressed for time). Add herbs and essential oils at your discretion according to personal preference and use.

Pray, dance, and be joyful as you stir and make your syrup. Think of all the good times, the times that were and the times that will be. Think of all the best things that you can imagine happening, the warmth of love and how it blossoms, and what it feels like to truly cherish something. Think about being totally uninhibited, being enthralled with and in love with yourself, think of warmth and family and home...Know that this simple recipe has been used in black households (and for jar workings) for generations.

If your feel that your petition for the opportunity to love yourself in a more fulfilling way requires a more significant sacrifice, feel free to use the more expensive alternatives of honey, molasses, or maple syrup instead of sugar syrup. If you prefer or need to use dry ingredients only, use plain sugar of any kind.

__Put Yourself In the Jar:__

- Go somewhere private (outdoors or indoors), taking all of your materials with you. Outside or inside, clear the area of leaves, debris, and flammables in front of you around 1 ft in all directions to ensure there are no accidents. Bring water and other safety materials just in case.

- Take a few minutes with your eyes closed, and in total silence, *listen.* Listen to the your music, the birds, wind, creek, chatter, and animals. Listen for the cars if you in a private place that is still in the city...listen to the ocean if you are by the coast. Listen to the people outside of your door. Find the rhythm and motion of the sound. Embrace it. This is your soundtrack for this ritual.
- Place your empty jar before you. If you want to smoke cleanse it first, you should do this now.
- Take the card and write a letter to yourself in the past asking to release any self-hate, self doubt, and other negative thoughts about your body, mind, and abilities from before.
- Turn the letter upside down and, using the other pen, write on top of your previous letter another letter. This letter should be to your future self, asking for Self-love, self-acceptance, and more positive circumstance with which to facilitate this. Ask to release all people who do not support this goal.
- Take the card and put your hair inside.
- Begin folding it *towards* yourself until it is small enough to be able to press down into the bottom of the jar and keep there. *While you fold* talk to your Ancestors about what you need to happen.
- Add drops of essential oils/ and a small amount of herbs at your discretion (research the use of each one to decide which to use more of.)
- Next, take the flower and make sure it can fit to almost the top of the jar. Place it inside, stem side down (it can be crooked, but the petals need to face up).
- Use the syrup and pour around the flower, envisioning the flower as yourself and the syrup as a bath of love, abundance, and well deserved blessings pouring over you. Fill the jar to the top, covering the flower.

- Tightly close the jar with the lid. Lift it and touch it to your mind, your heart, and your womb, saying each time, "I accept and love myself completely".
- Put one tea light on top of the jar, and light it, talking about your self-esteem, your relationship with yourself and what you would like to happen as a result of your self-confidence. Be thorough, have a conversation. Allow the wax to drip down around the jar.
- Begin to arrange and light each tea light in a spiral shape blooming out from the jar. In between each light, arrange your flowers and leaves. These tealights should remain in their small holder. *Make sure your area is clear of flammables!*
- As you create this little altar, *hum*. Let the song come naturally from your heart *or* let it be one that you have known all along...perhaps one that you were taught by an elder that you have once known. Let your song go in the rhythm of nature around you.

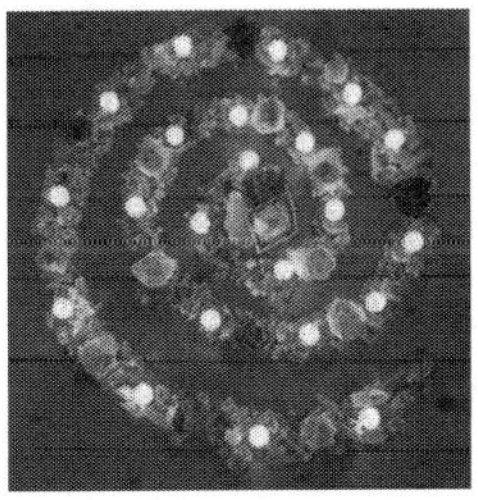

- When you have finished the altar, sit before your altar with your hands uplifted, opened, or in prayer.
- Finish your time there when it feels natural to do so.
- Clean up your candles when they burn out (if you cannot wait for this, wait as long as you can) and leave the flora to the earth. Put your jar by your altar.
- Find a routine time to sit by your jar (such as every Sunday or every full moon) and focus your energy on yourself awareness, self-love, and self-care. Look through the jar at the sun and the moon and pray heartfelt prayer.

  Take note of any changes, good or bad. Focus on improvements in your attitude towards yourself and how to continue that momentum. Place yourself in situations that give your self esteem a better chance as you heal.

  Cut off people who bring you down--learn how to use the block button online and on the phone, and use those tools with no shame! Get restraining orders if necessary. Release that which isn't serving you and recognize it is not your duty to piggy-back everyone who catches eyes on you to the finish line of life!

**To modify this jar for sweetening and love jars for other people, you can modify ingredients and intent to fit your needs.

Notes on Self-Love Jar

Date/Time:	

2nd Monday -
Know Ya Womb

The word "<u>womb</u>" is synonymous with the uterus--it is the organ where offspring are conceived and in which they gestate before birth. But the word also has a second definition... It is also **the place in which *anything* is formed or produced**. Your womb is a place of great creative energy that can form or produce just about any emotion, asset, or circumstance you can imagine (and even some that you can't).

<u>Punani</u>, is a word that means "heavenly flower" and comes from the Old Hawaiian words *pua* meaning "blossom" and *nani* meaning "glory,

splendor, heavenly". Today the beautiful term that refers to the vulva has been adopted by many English speakers across the United States and beyond…(the vulva is the external parts of the vagina that can be seen).

Proverbs, you might know, are folk-talk... a wise thought or some good advice based on common sense or experience by the average person.

Between these definitions, the real secret to Punani Proverbs lies because in truth, your punani has so much more to teach you than many might realize.

The womb is a powerhouse of creation that goes far beyond baby making, as beautiful and amazing as that is by itself. It is a vortex of energy within that can be used in whichever direction you need for whatever you desire. When you are able to specify your thoughts and direction regarding this energy, that is where your magic can really begin to bloom.

You are not your body, but your soul *did* choose your body. Isn't it time to really, truly embrace that? Isn't it time to be unapologetically knowledgeable and proud of your body? Isn't it time to use that energy to place yourself smack dab into the life you have always wanted, the life you deserve….your (dare I say it) *birthright*? In the case of how you use this powerful energy within you, your feelings about yourself absolutely do matter.

Starting from a more physical/ scientific perspective, let's find out what you already know! **Without looking at any references (including your own body), label the reproductive system below**. Do your best...this is just for fun to challenge brain and utilize your current knowledge. It will also be a fun way to look back on your growth as you learn more. If you can't think of a name...make one up! Block the other pictures if you need to, just be sure to relax and have fun.

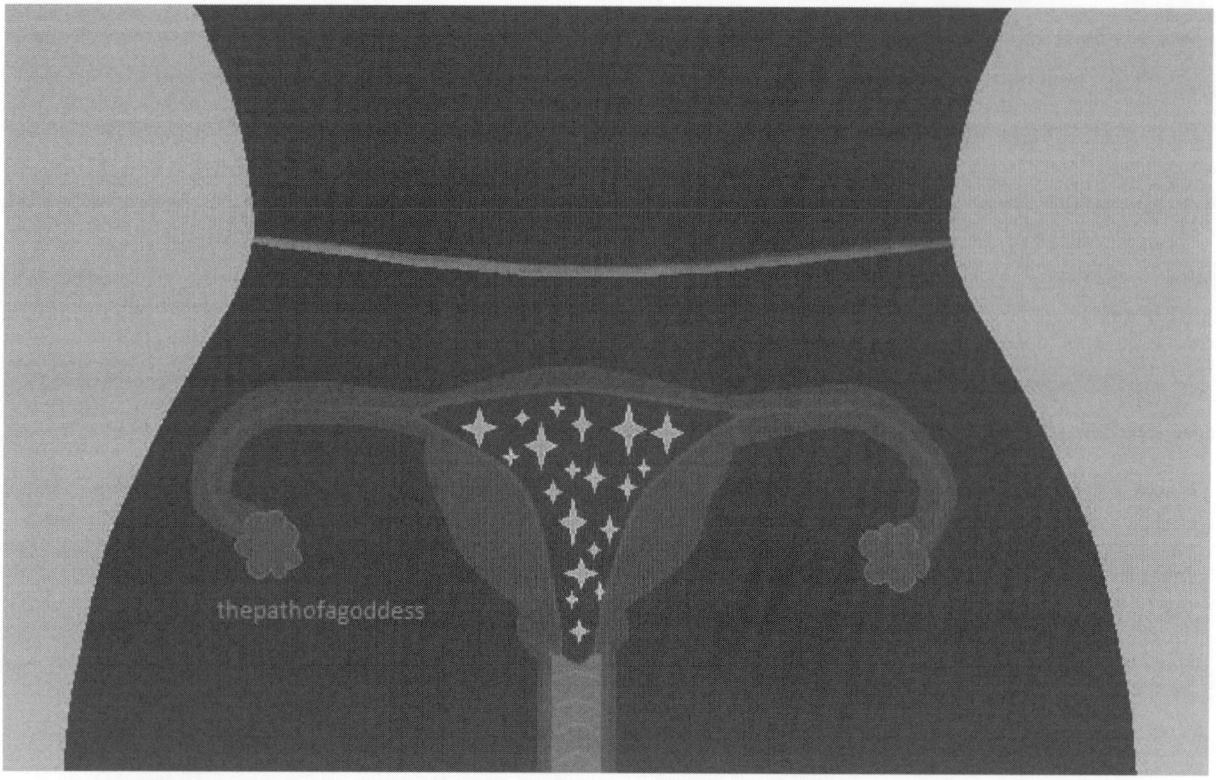

Answers:

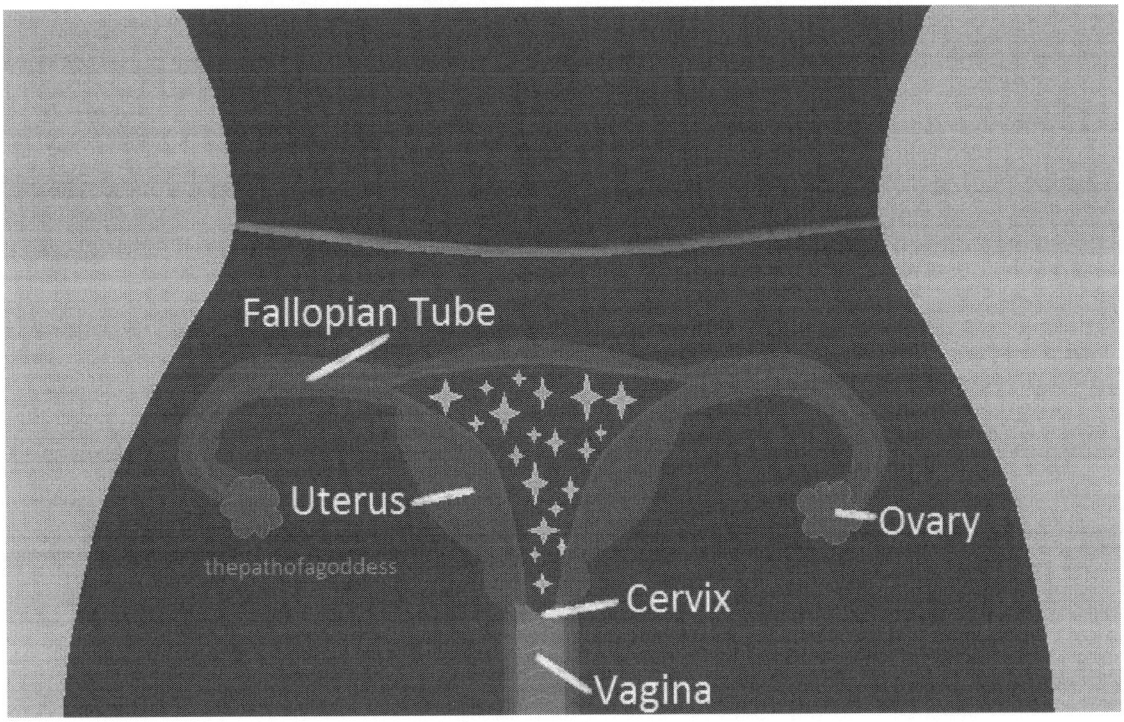

Personal Study:

(Use this section to write what you know, but also what you know about your own womb personally. Does one of your ovaries ache more than the other? Do you know what that means when that happens? Does a massage or other home remedy help? Feel free to draw sketches, write reminders, or explain in your own terms.)

Fallopian Tubes: The tubes along which the egg travels from the ovaries to the uterus.

Ovaries: The reproductive organ in which ova (eggs) are produced.

Uterus: The organ where offspring are conceived and gestate before birth. Also called the womb.

Cervix: The narrow passage forming the lower end of the uterus. The lower part bulges slightly into the vagina.

Vagina: The muscular tube leading from the external genitals (between the labia minora) to the cervix.

Vulva: The external (female) genitals.

Notes/Thoughts:

3rd Monday

Body Love, Pussy Love

Stand before your mirror and stare yourself in the eyes with love, care, and respect. Enjoy what you see. Slowly undress yourself, pulling each layer off with tender fingers, not rushing anything about the process.

Keep your movements smooth and steady, try not to jerk or lose your grace. Unleash each inch of your skin luxuriously, allow your hands to caress your body as you reveal it to the air.

When you are finished allow yourself to relish in the transition. **This is the sacred and powerful ritual of Undressing with Purpose.** It is the cherishing of your actions, movements, and transitions to even the smallest flick. It is the gaining of control of your body through the noticing and adoring of your body. It is considering your body to be a temple-- Sacred Space. It is a reminder to add this sacred touch to all of the things you choose to do, every day.

For this particular Challenge, we continue on once undressed. When you are ready, lounge yourself back on to a comfortable sofa or bed nearby. If you'd like, take a video so you can watch yourself later, see your hands touch your skin and witness your response in a new way.

Using a smooth oil that can be used all over the body (such as coconut, olive, avocado, walnut, vitamin E, or similar), begin this challenge with a light facial massage. Try to relax away all of the tension that builds and rests there. Allow it to release and melt away. Re-apply oil throughout the small ritual as needed.

Move your hands down to your neck and shoulders. Gently work at the knots on there out to the best of your abilities. Bring your hands to your chest and massage thoroughly, being sure your nipples receive nourishment as well.

Rub oil all over your abdomen, and spend time massaging the womb for a little while too. This is about four fingers down from your belly button. Massaging your womb should be firm, but should definitely not hurt or harm you. If you feel you need further assistance, consider hiring a practitioner who is trained in womb massage.

When you are satisfied, begin to rub the crease on the outer creases of your vagina… Smooth your skin luxuriously using the pads of your fingertips to apply as pressure and warmth. Hold and rub with your palm. **Enjoy the time you spend with yourself.** Relax.

Actually take mental note of your likes and dislikes....Write them down below later. As you learn more, remember to combe back and add to the list.

My Punani Likes:	My Punani Dislikes:

Notes/Thoughts:

4th Monday

Vulva Sketch

The vulva is the outside view of the vagina. Again Undress with Purpose, but this time, lay back with a mirror between your legs, allowing you to see your entire beautiful sacred space in all of its unique and sexy glory!

Take time to breath slowly and deeply, moving your eyes slowly to focus on each inch of skin visually. Look at how your hair grows and your senses respond to being watched. Look at where the light reflects...focus on where you know from memory is the most sensitive of spaces. Notice which parts change color, where you have beauty marks and where you may differ from what is considered "normal" or common…

Smile at this wonder--this garden of glory--your body. You are beautiful and unique just the way you are. *You* are normal. What you see in pictures or TV is often simply one powerful person's opinion repeated and broadcast over and over again to millions of people. It is not accurate to most people, not only yourself. *You* are the most perfect of all creations. All genitalia are "normal". What you see before you is in all power and right *yours* and really, should you choose to Reject All Laws of Man, it is a very powerful gift to have been given indeed.

Breathe deep this scent that is uniquely yours. Do not believe it will change...the base scent of your pussy is yours and yours alone! No one else on this earth will ever smell like the scent you exude from your Sacred Chamber! This is a gift of yours--it can attract powerful people, experiences, and treasure into your life.

Think about your relationship with the appearance and smell of your vulva. Has it impacted you? How?

Have you ever been shy about the look or smell of your vagina? Why?

Have you ever felt particularly satisfied with the pussy you have?

Do you take time to pamper your punani's outward appearance and aesthetic? What are ways you can add to your punani pampering routine?

Using a pencil, sketch your vulva as accurately as you can, taking your time:

When you are done, feel free to outline in black ink, and/or color.

Finally, go ahead and pamper your vulva for being such a wonderful model! Since you are already exposed and feeling the breeze, let your punani catch some sun too. Position yourself outside somewhere private, or by a sunny window in your home. Let the sun touch your skin for a few minutes (not too long, especially at first!) and feel the delicious warmth. Then, clean yourself, freshen up, and put on fresh cotton panties.

Thoughts:

5th Monday

Vulva Knowledge

Today, we will label again...this time, the different parts of the vulva that come together to make one beautiful sculpture of art right there between your legs!

Again, let's just label from memory or even wishful thinking all by yourself...if you did particularly poorly last round, you can think about soliciting the help of a close friend you trust to only look at as much of the workbook as you are willing to share. See if the two of you combined can figure it all out!

Use pictures of your own and other people's vaginas as reference to continue learning and growing with your knowledge and comfort of the punani.

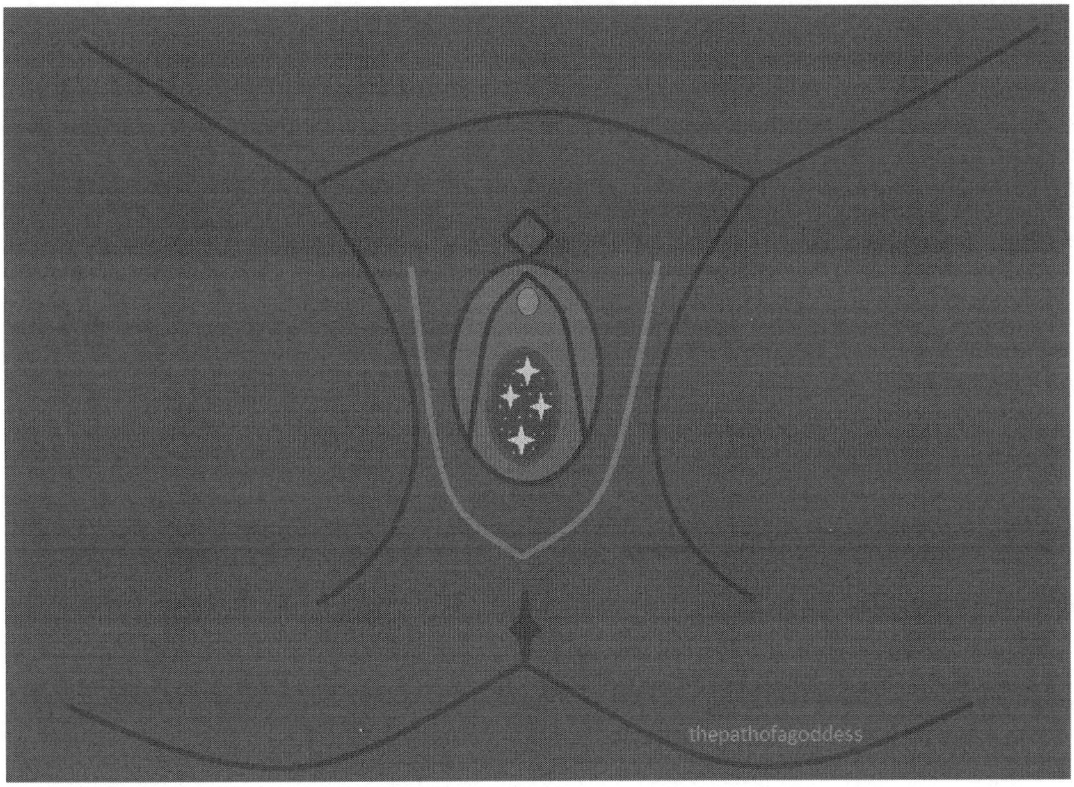
thepathofagoddess

Answers:

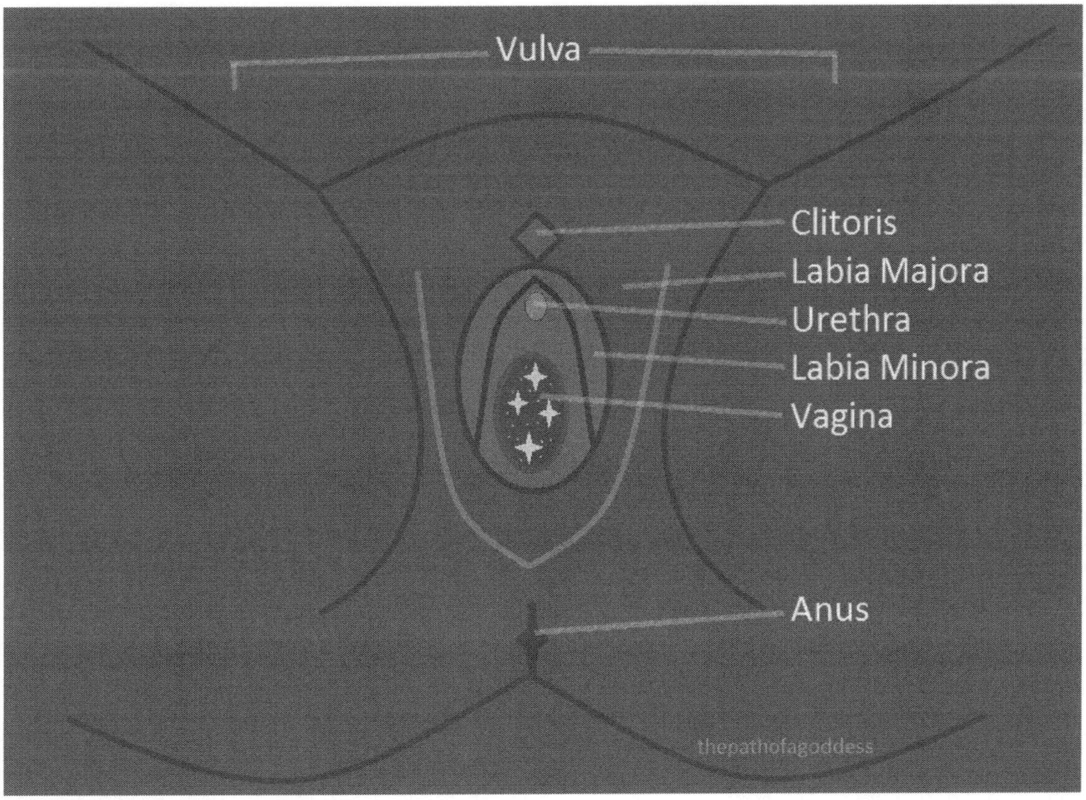
Vulva
Clitoris
Labia Majora
Urethra
Labia Minora
Vagina
Anus
thepathofagoddess

Notes:

6th Monday

Womb Meditation

Have you ever practiced silence with your womb? Give your womb time to speak, let any grievances be aired. *Does* your womb have anything to say? Has the same mantra been repeating over and over, but you haven't been listening? Do you even understand your womb's words when they are being spoken?

Ways The Womb Speaks:

- Small, fleeting, "ghost" pains or aches.
- Serious cramping. Can be continuous or occur on one or the other ovary.
- Stopping all menstruation and/or bleeding.
- Spotting, light or heavy.
- Bleeding continuously.
- Discharge (communication through color, texture, type).
- Sudden thought in the mind about what should be done about an issue, seemingly from nowhere.
- Cold or empty feeling deep within. Disconnected.
- Warm or serene feelings emanating from the womb center.
- Interest, excitement, or sexual arousal, even in nonsexual situations.
- Other personal signs you may notice that are unique to your womb.

Has your womb been speaking to you, and you did not realize? Do you know what your womb is asking for and telling you with each of these changes?

Undress with Purpose and find a comfortable way to rest (sit, lay down, recline) and rest both hands on your womb.

Make a personal chart for yourself below to help yourself remember...Fill it out from memory the best you can today, but be sure to come back and add more details as you come to learn more!

Physical Symptom:	What My Womb Means Is:

7th Monday

Word Search

1) Today, we search for the right words, in different ways. First, a traditional word search puzzle using vocabulary we have been learning so far:

S	A	J	E	D	P	B	L	F	B	S	L	B	P	U	S	S	Y	S	H	Q
T	H	G	O	V	M	T	E	E	A	U	O	U	S	H	I	A	E	S	A	U
R	B	E	O	O	O	U	G	C	N	D	P	E	P	Q	T	B	W	E	M	N
E	C	A	W	Y	N	L	R	Y	Y	W	V	C	R	B	B	S	M	N	R	M
T	A	E	W	N	Y	E	F	P	U	R	H	H	O	V	Z	R	S	L	T	Z
C	W	V	R	V	D	D	O	L	U	S	I	Z	V	S	W	D	M	L	X	K
H	Q	A	A	V	H	S	M	C	E	F	N	G	E	F	A	F	W	E	H	Q
M	S	U	N	A	I	S	E	C	C	S	O	S	R	E	C	A	U	W	P	Y
A	Q	L	P	T	D	X	R	S	Z	R	Y	F	B	S	J	R	X	P	U	Q
R	U	A	I	E	L	C	R	I	C	R	E	T	S	I	S	O	H	U	N	Y
K	A	V	N	S	U	R	E	T	U	V	S	N	Y	G	Q	N	V	M	A	A
S	E	R	N	C	J	D	E	L	U	I	O	A	G	O	A	I	C	M	N	D
Q	A	T	O	K	E	T	O	L	A	C	Y	O	D	J	V	M	U	I	I	N
A	C	N	W	J	A	S	V	W	L	B	E	L	L	Y	D	A	N	C	E	O
E	G	G	I	M	A	A	T	I	U	R	E	T	H	R	A	I	R	W	M	M
Q	H	P	I	G	S	M	T	O	B	C	B	Q	S	O	H	B	I	Y	N	A
Q	W	T	S	I	A	O	A	C	R	J	O	B	O	L	G	A	L	C	L	Y
O	N	K	X	V	R	V	I	I	X	S	C	F	N	L	T	L	W	N	H	N
I	J	W	X	I	Z	J	V	D	B	Z	M	M	M	S	M	S	P	C	E	I
D	N	U	S	X	F	F	I	R	V	A	T	O	P	Y	E	N	O	H	N	Z
E	J	Z	O	Y	A	Q	E	Q	M	V	L	D	L	D	C	C	O	C	L	J

Checklist:

• Anus • Cervix • Egg • Labia Majora • Punani Proverbs • Sacred • Stretch Marks • Uterus • Waistbeads • Yoga • Belly Dance • Clitoris • Honey Pot • Labia Minora • Vagina	• Pussy • Self-Love • Monday • Wellness • Yoni • Body Positive • Curves • Intimate • Ovary • Rolls • Sister Circle • Urethra • Vulva • Womb • Ancestors

2) With these words in mind, we are going to go do a small "word search" silent meditation. Go somewhere where you can lay or sit comfortably, undisturbed. Close your eyes and practice silence and spending time with your own mind for the next 10-30 minutes.

Begin by breathing deeply, using the full capacity of your lungs. Give one deep breath for every year that you have been alive and, with each breath, relax further into position for your meditation.

Listen to your body and attempt to channel messages from it for this entire time. Any messages that come to mind--colors, single words, sentences, or otherwise can all be meditated upon or considered.

Immediately when you finish (or as soon as you can afterwards), jot down notes and quick doodles and express yourself below of any thoughts that came up during your time of silence ruminating on the words and themes from the word search:

3) Use half of the boxes below to draw pictures of a person enjoying and accepting their womb and body, flaws and all. In the remaining boxes, write short poems, haikus, single words, or a couple of sentences to accompany them, using the word search list and your own notes above to aid you.

The Belly

If you are a human being with a womb you have probably realized by now that your what you eat can and often does effect just about every facet of your life.

Your womb and your belly have a *very* special relationship, as you are probably aware.

One of the first ways that come to mind is how we are always urged to suck ourselves in. Be smaller, shorter, skinnier. Don't be or do too much. Only be or do too much in this exact way. Having a belly never seems to be the right way, and yet most of us have them. We are judged for the flatness of stomach, skinny teenage bodies placed on a pedestal by upper class and eurocentric society...and so we suck it in, in, in. Some of us don't even realize we do it anymore. Do you hunch your shoulders too?

I'm here to ask you to stop. Allow your belly and womb to *relax*.

The womb sits directly below all of the intestines--which are stuffed full of whatever it is you have chosen to eat in the past hours, days, and sometimes even weeks.

Factually speaking, some foods just plain take longer to digest than others. Vegetables and fruits that are high in fiber move through the system quickly, whereas foods like meats and dairy tend to remain clogged in the system for days, weeks, and yes months at a time.

Anyone who has smelled raw meat or dairy that is even an hour passed expiration understands that this food gets very foul, very quickly, and it's not something you want to imagine building up on your intestines, causing you to only go to the bathroom for a bowel movement once a day, or even every few days or weeks.

While the intestines are busy growing heavier and heavier with slowly digesting matter--almost 100% of which is known to be exposed to cancer causing hormones, growths, and unclean, unsafe living conditions throughout life--the womb is stuck bearing the brunt of this accumulating weight.

For many, it stays in this strained position for years or decades, and then they wonder why they have issue becoming pregnant, and having or tracking a regular cycle. **A diet change won't make your pussy magically taste like strawberries (nor should your pussy *ever* taste like anything but punani!), but it will fill your life with wellness which is much more healthy and practical.**

<u>Foods That Weigh The Intestines Down:</u>

- Meat
- Dairy
- Milk chocolate
- Deep fried foods
- White grains/starches

- Alcohol

<u>Foods That Help The Intestines Lighten Up:</u>

- Fiber (lentils, avocado, chickpeas, beans, lentils, peas, chia seeds)
- Omega 3 Fatty Foods (flax & chia seeds, walnuts, soybeans)
- Fruits (prunes, pears, apples, fig, citrus
- Vegetables (sweet potato, dark leafy greens)
- Whole grains

Consider also getting an enema done both at home or professionally if the health or spiritual situation you suffer is serious.

Once your diet and intestines are brought under control, you can work on posture and other wellness techniques, but never go back to flexing all day and night. At least give yourself 9 hours to breath fully daily.

Notes:

Discharge

Okay let's start with the facts. Discharge happens. Most people with vaginas have discharge. Some do not. Many people increase discharge during pregnancy and other phases of life. This is all within the range of "normal". You are most likely to see discharge while wiping in the bathroom, looking at the crotch of your underwear, or when having sex/masturbating.

Signs of Healthy Discharge:	• It is clear, white, or off-white in color • Sometimes brown discharge is seen following the period. • Stretchier discharge (often clear) usually indicates fertility. • Watery discharge is common, especially after exercise. • Usually around 1 teaspoon daily, but can vary due to individual and increase when sexually aroused.
Take Notice If Your Discharge:	• Your period has irregular bleeding or spotting. • You notice your natural (usual/most common) odor has changed recently. Everyone's vagina gives off a different odor...this is why it is *so* important for you to get to know your own body!
Go To The Doctor When:	• Changes in discharge color, such as green or yellow.

	• The smell is consistently different, or has become unpleasant • The texture changes to a cheesey or foamy one. • Your period is consistently irregular. • You think you might have an STD • You have fever along with pain in the belly region. • You experience discomfort (itching, rashes, sores, pain) • Sudden changes in quantity of discharge (unless you are aroused).

Healing Toxic Discharge

So we know that discharge is a healthy and normal thing...in fact, "healthy" and "normal" range from barely any ever, to a steady amount daily!

There are a few ways you can help your vaginal health on your own, however as with all physical ailments there comes a time when you do need to see a doctor for some form of treatment.

No matter what, when you have an infection it is important to keep your vagina clean. Change your diet at the time, and refuse all foods which will not heal you if you are serious about fixing the infection yourself. Don't use anything but a very mild soap and warm water to wash your vulva and vaginal canal. Avoid "feminine products" such as douches, rubs, lotions, sprays and similar. Always wipe from front to back and wear 100% cotton underwear at all times, and *no underwear* to bed.

We will look at some of the causes, and ways to heal them here:

Bacterial Vaginosis	A vaginal infection, BV usually requires doctor intervention. Before going, you can try to heal it yourself with incredibly good hygiene, a small detox routine, and making a personal mixture of coconut and other healing oils of your choosing. Wear only cotton underwear or nothing at all during this time and go to the doctors if it doesn't appear to get better in a few days.
Hormonal Birth Control	Birth Control (BC) affects your hormones and the natural release of blood during your period. The only way to heal your discharge from BC is to stop taking the hormones and find a natural method of BC such as the diaphragm.
Douches, toxic bubble baths and bath bombs	The vagina is a self cleaning organ that does *not* need to be helped with a douche. To heal from a douche, rinse the vagina with warm water and wash with a very mild soap. You may use oils on the outside and inside of the vagina to massage, but keep it light and do not use so much that you clog the pores. When using bubble baths and bath bombs be sure to buy those with natural ingredients, and to pee after taking a bath with them.
Sexually Transmitted Diseases and Infections	STDs and STIs can cause the pelvis to become inflamed. They require

	doctor intervention and prescribed antibiotic and antiviral drugs. Be sure to get tested with your doctor regularly if you are not in a committed relationship, and even if you are slightly suspicious of your partner. You never know and it is better safe than sorry. It is always better to know what your STI status is than to ignore the problem and have to face harder consequences down the road. There is nothing wrong with contracting one, and they are in fact incredibly common. Always be honest, above all with yourself, about your STI status.
Yeast Infection	A yeast infection might heal from cleanliness and coconut oil mixed with a small amount of diluted tea tree oil, but it usually needs more. Antifungal creams for yeast infections can be found over the counter, allowing it to be easily treated at home. Many also find adding half a cup apple cider vinegar to their baths helps relieve symptoms. If the infection does not heal with your over the counter medicine, go to the doctor.
Vaginal Atrophy	Natural lubricants such as jojoba oil, coconut oil, aloe vera, and vitamin e are used to moisturize and heal the thinning of the vaginal walls, also

	called atrophy. Giving up smoking cigarettes, being sexually active, and keeping well hydrated can all aid with vaginal atrophy symptoms. If your symptoms are too terrible, your doctor might suggest estrogen creams.
Foreign Objects	Check for a foreign object, such as an old forgotten tampon or sponge! It sounds crazy, but it could happen when you least expect it, and removal as well as washing out your vagina (and keeping it clean and open to the air for a few days) can heal this issue.
Diabetes	When your diabetes is poorly controlled, your immune systems responses become hindered and less likely to react in time of need. You can help prevent this by remaining as healthy as possible with diabetes, wearing cotton underwear, and maintaining excellent hygiene. Be sure to dry your body really well after bathing or showering.

Notes:

Cysts

Ovarian cysts and fibroid cysts are small sacks of fluid that can begin to accumulate on the ovaries. Typically this is caused by a follicle not opening to release an egg when it was time. Because of this, womb bearers who have regular cycles are actually more prone to getting them, and in fact many do create and lose them regularly and without problem. Only about 8% of wombs with cysts prior to menopause require treatments to remove them.

Most cysts are small, do not cause symptoms, and are not malevolent. They can grow quietly only to be found much later. Many just go away naturally, or with basic herbal remedies as medicine. Others do require surgery and other more invasive measures to truly heal from.

If you suspect you have cysts on your ovaries, consult your doctor! They will be able to give you a medical exam and diagnose you if you do. They will be able to determine what kind of cysts you have and if the condition is an emergency.

Also consult yourself. Use your hands and hold your womb. Ask what you, specifically, need to do to heal what is hurting you.

Causes:

- Smoking cigarettes
- Overconsumption of meat and dairy
- Hormonal problems (sometimes ones that can be regulated after giving birth or breastfeeding)
- Depression, guilt, or stress that has built up to the point of physical symptoms
- Hormonal birth control/ovulation drugs
- Pregnancy: Sometimes one will grow to support the egg after conception, and remain through until the placenta has formed.
- Obesity related health issues.

Symptoms:

- Pain in the lower abdomen/position of the cyst (sharp or dull and without a period)
- Pressure
- Pain during bowel movements
- Swelling
- Breast tenderness
- Bloating
- Pain during sex
- Weight gain
- Menstrual changes, Irregular periods
- Infertility

Severe Symptoms: (could indicate cyst is ruptured or broken, go to Dr.)

- Pain with fever and vomiting
- Sudden and severe abdominal pain
- Faintness/dizziness/weakness

- Rapid breathing
- Heavy bleeding

Healing:

When choosing to naturally heal a physical malady such as cysts, dedication to your healing is crucial. It can feel frustrating to hear what feels like simple bullet points over and over, but the truth is not as complex as it might seem. In all honesty your healing takes *as much or more dedication* towards discipline and wellness that you had towards undisciplined lifestyle before. **The steps that led you to this point must be retraced to the best of your abilities.**

For some, this is easy. For others who have been running strong in the wrong direction for a long time, this will be more difficult.

- If you are serious about this, you will eliminate the meat and dairy from your diet. You will not focus on your size or weight so much as you will focus on your *health*. You will focus on your overall wellness and choices. You will eliminate that which clearly isn't serving you. You will research to understand
- You will focus on the emotional, mental, and spiritual baggage you have been holding on to for so long. You will let go of what happened to you 30 years ago, 10 years ago, 5 years ago. With steady practice, you will learn the art of staying centered and serene, despite what might go on in your surroundings.
- You will release the reliance on hormonal birth control and all of the convenience that it gives you, because you will recognize that blood clots, cysts, infertility, irregular or debilitating periods, and other forms of early illness and death are not actually convenient at all. You will recognize that covering up symptoms is not healing them. You will find another way.

As you make each of these choices, your womb will heal. How quick the healing is depends heavily on how large your dedication and discipline truly is.

Finally, I wish to remind you that surgery is indeed sometimes necessary, even for cysts! **If your cysts require surgical removal it is still imperative that you follow the above guidelines. Your cysts will continue to recur until the true root cause of them is resolved**, be that cause physical or spiritual.

Notes:

Punanilates

Many of you are probably familiar with the pelvic floor, especially if you have ever carried a child within your womb...it is the part of your body that threatens to utterly betray you at night when you cannot seem to get to the bathroom quickly enough to pee!

If you have no clue anything about the pelvic floor, and can't picture where it might be, go recheck the diagram on the first Monday of the 7 Monday Challenge! Also look up pictures online. Close your eyes and imagine your womb in your mind's eye-- feel it and imagine it glowing gold.

Today, pelvic floor exercises are commonly called "kegels" or "kegel exercise", but I refuse to (of all the nicknames) refer to such a personal part of my body after the last name of an old white man who as per usual didn't invent anything and took a lot of credit, so….

For the sake of this book, let's call them the Punanilates (Punani Pilates), and continue on!

a. b.

- Stand straight. Putting your arms in front of you for balance, bend your knees and lower your body down into a squatting position-- feet flat with calves and thighs touching. Keep length in the spine as it remains straight and put the pressure in your heels.
  This may take time for you to accomplish...if you cannot squat with your feet flat on the ground, use a rolled mat under each heel to rest on. Maintain pressure throughout the heels.
- Start with figure (a), previously shown. Closing your eyes, see your golden pelvic floor glowing in your mind again. Imagine both the front and back of your pelvis moving towards each other, with your vaginal

opening being where both are trying to connect.
Squeeze together the best you can...though your mind might be able to see what you want, your body will probably not be able to respond correctly the first 4 or so times you try.
Start with 10 reps, work your way up slowly.

- Now look at the squatting figure (b). This time when you envision your pelvic floor, imagine the two sides, right and left, pulling together to the center. This is a slightly different feeling that activates other muscles within your vagina and pelvis, allowing for a thorough pelvic workout. Again, start with only 5-10 reps so as not to overdo it or strain your body or womb, and slowly increase every week.

These "simple" steps might feel confusing or like they are doing nothing at first, but assuredly they will feel more and more powerful as time goes on.

A brilliant, ancient technique to enhance your Punanilates is to invest in a crystal yoni egg. Insert them while exercising your pelvis, and keep them in throughout the day. Smaller eggs take more effort to keep inside, while larger ones take less strain and are more suited for beginners.

Learn more about these womb crystals and how to choose them in the "Matrilineal Meditations" section.

Cold Womb

The womb responds to warmth...this is something that our ancient Ancestors knew. Today you will see online articles touting "padsicles" for postpartum, but long term, the choice of warm over cold is always best for the punani especially after a large event (both physical and emotional).

A common and old remedy for initial treatment and pain relief is a hot \rice sock or hot water bottle, and this usually works. The womb is naturally heated by the hormone *progesterone*, however there are times when the uterine lining doesn't respond, or this natural method (for a variety of reasons) is not enough.

Cold tightens all of the muscles in the body, and slows blood flow. Your energy is slowed as well, and you can also be affected spiritually if you remain without addressing the cause of your Cold Womb for long enough. Take it seriously if you feel either physically, emotionally, or spiritually that your womb is cold.

Physical and Spiritual Causes:

- Depression
- PTSD
- Sitting/Standing on a cold floor regularly
- Not dressing appropriately for the weather
- Abuse/ Attachment to an abuser
- Wearing wet clothes too long
- Stress/ Feeling the world is on your shoulders
- Feeling abandoned/ Alone
- Drinking too many cold beverages
- Being overly tired

Warming up the womb can be as simple as creating and consuming a hearty, warm, wholesome meal, with a little bit of spice and flavors in it, and a whole lot of love. You can allow your feet to soak in a warm foot soak, or take a hot shower. A spiritual bath with hot water to pour over the head would be excellent as well. Heating pads, stones, rice socks, and hot water bottles are easy to access and perfect for relaxation (stones can be heated in a crockpot or oven on low heat, and should be wrapped in cloth...you can find out more about them in the "Postpartum Rituals" section of the workbook). Finally, you may need to release people and situations that are not serving you, but definitely can be released.

Start utilizing these methods for around 15-20 minutes at a time, initially, as often as needed for personal wellness. Certain issues will require much deeper remedy and even professional guidance than others for you. Remember that your Ancestors are with you as you journey on this path of healing, wellness and recovery. Also remember that the community is with you and cherishes you and your needs. Do not be afraid to ask for help! Whatever path you need to take, never forget to utilize self care along the way. It is amazing what, even in the darkest of times, a healing ritual can do for you.

Rice Bag

A rice bag is one of the easiest heating packs that people make at home and for each other.

- Use the longest tube sock you can find (but not a knee high sock!)
- Fill the sock with 4-6 cups of rice
- Knot the end closed.
- Put a few drops of essential oil (such as lavender) on the sock.
- Heat in the microwave for 2-3 minutes every time you need some warmth on your womb or back during your period or any other time!

Hot Water "Bottle"

Hot water bottles are can be bought for cheap, but they can also be created at home! These are excellent for people who do not have a microwave.

- Heat water on the stove until steaming hot
- Soak some dish towels in the water
- Place the dish towels inside of a plastic lockable bag
- Wrap in a t-shirt or towel….if you use this method often you might find it in your favor to sew, crochet, or knit a bag just for this purpose.

Notes:

Part Two: In The Garden of My Womb

(although I like it)

Honey Pot Chronicles #2

A womb grew there.
Wild.
And should you ever ask if
there is a need for taking the gardening shears to
prune petals, leaves, branch and thorn
the womb would ask,
"Why do you mind?"
The spirit of it is,
some bushes are best left to grow away
where their thorns can't cut anyone,
including oneself.
And others sometimes need a gentle touch
to nudge them this way
or that...

A womb grows there,
uninhibited by expectation or fear,
it grows and creates and thrives--
A womb grows there
centered within a core

nestled neat, its roots have spread deep into each crevice of muscle & bone
and now...was there ever a time when this garden did not feed you?
This space once empty, accepted the first seed and
a womb flourished there...
Wild.

Bonding with your womb *isn't* always about making the so-called "perfect" choice at every turn! Some would have you believe that if you are not perfectly disciplined as a breatharian-herbal-elemental-witch who caters to the Moon Cycle, you are a fraud or not healed. This is a complete farce.

Your ritual, *your* connection with your root chakra and womb power is about respecting tradition *and* respecting personal needs. It's about respecting your body's indulgences, respecting who you want to be, your life path, who you are right now and who you've been….It's even about who you evolve into within your own personal growth. Discipline is necessary for certain levels of healing and training, this is very true. But any person can create a sacred and spiritual journey within context of their world, and with their own personal creative womb and sexual energy!

What are some of your "guilty" indulgences? Do you ever hide any of your indulgences?

Why do you feel negatively about indulging yourself? Are they unsafe, embarrassing, or prone to judgment?

How can you overcome these feelings?

Womb Art Portfolio

This challenge asks you to creatively consider your womb. Compare your power center--your sacred seat--to the cosmos, nature, and other parts of the world around you. Come to see your body as a piece of the universe that has been gifted to you to enjoy, thrive with, and take care of.

With a mirror and a timer, stare at your vulva for 5 minutes while you play music or ambient sounds you enjoy. Turn away from the mirror afterwards and draw your own vulva *from memory* using *only 10 lines.*

Draw your womb using only items found in space. Write 3 sentences relating the galaxies and your womb together.

Using flowers, draw your own womb in the state of health it is in. Label each flower and explanation the symbolism behind why you chose it.

Use 4 colors (marker, watercolor, etc) and 3 shapes to draw your own vagina (inside and out). You may need to let one layer dry before doing the next.

Squat outside with no underwear on (wear a maxi dress or skirt if you are worried about onlookers). Relax and meditate allowing energy to flow throughout your body, straight through your womb, down to the toes and up into the brain. Come back inside after 10+ minutes and draw what your yoni felt at the time.

Draw your vulva using only *one* line. Be as abstract or concrete as you care to be.

Draw one thing you have had inside your vagina. (crystal egg, sex toy, body part, air etc)

Draw one thing you have had inside your womb. (pregnancy, idea, etc)

Draw one thing you want to have inside of your vagina in the future.

Sacred Movement Sundays

Every Sunday for the next 10 weeks, choose one song and simply move to it, allowing your spiritual nature to connect. Don't worry about looking good or perfect. Do not fear embarrassment or a lack of perfection. This practice isn't about being the best or displaying yourself to the most people (though by all means get a witness and share your journey if that helps you) but rather about embracing ourselves and connecting fully with our vessel. The best way to become better at movement is to simply do it and express yourself...there is no need to become a professional first.

The songs can be any of your choosing, but overall your song choice should be varied in genre, artist, mood, and theme. Choose a wide range of emotions --sensuality, anger, love, lust, disappointment, sadness, and inhibition. Then, draw, journal, or write a poem about that movement experience.

Song:	Notes:

Phases of Menstruation

When we hear people talk about periods, it's either the blessed feminine cycle of the goddess of the river red flowing nirvana...or it's the dreaded visit from Auntie Flo, here to wreck havoc on your favorite undies and sex life.

The energy of your moon cycle is that of abundance, overflow, sensuality, harmony, creation, love, tenderness, and decadence. It is also one of winding down and release. When we hear people talk about periods, it's either the blessed feminine cycle of the goddess of the river red flowing nirvana...or it's the dreaded visit from Auntie Flo, here to wreck havoc on your favorite undies and sex life.

The energy of your moon cycle is that of abundance, overflow, sensuality, harmony, creation, love, tenderness and decadence. It is also one of winding down and release.

It's important to chart your cycle for more reasons than fertility. The actual bleeding portion of your cycle is only one part of the month long process. Through it, you ebb and flow throughout moods and feelings and can utilize each of these phases to your advantage throughout your personal life.

It's important to chart your cycle for more reasons than fertility. The actual bleeding portion of your cycle is only one part of the month long process. Through it, you ebb and flow throughout moods and feelings and can utilize each of these phases to your advantage throughout your personal life.

There are **four basic feminine archetypes that have lasted straight through to modern times--The Maiden, The Mother, The Enchantress, and the Crone**. Each of these spirits resides within each of us...for some it is easier to access one than it is to access the other, but each has a gift to share and a time to be utilized.

I am sure we all know someone who appears to rest easily in just one of these archetypes at all times, but in actuality, we all cycle through them both through life, circumstance and through menstruation. Each of these spirits is within us and can be called upon when needed.

In the following pages, we will relate these spirits to our Moon Cycle, as they have been done throughout time.

The Maiden

Just after the period (the time of bleeding) ends is considered the time of the Maiden--also called the "follicular phase". This isn't a reference to your sexual status….in origin the word "virgin" actually was an ancient term that referred to a very uninhibited and independent womb bearer. I am talking about the *boldness of youth.*

The Maiden knows what they need and are willing to reach or ask for it. They are confident in their ability to do so--and this confidence holds a *lot* of weight. The Maiden has a *ton* of ideas...they bounce around in their head at all times. They know each idea is worth a million dollars and passionately throws themselves into the work that is required because the Maiden is rarely tired or burned out. With wild abandon they juggle a hundred impossible tasks, running on nothing but the pure fire within their soul. They are a force to be reckoned with and an opportunity to be taken.

Though this time of the cycle can still feel sluggish, it is an excellent time for empowerment. The Maiden can be brought out through dressing to perfection, a photo shoot, an act of wild impulse, or similar...this is a time of enjoying pampering and seduction. Maidens aren't the type for regrets--they are the type to learn and move on.

Don’t get caught in endless creation--starting, starting, but never finishing. Use this phase to prepare your outward creation and expression, as well as catapult you into where you need to go.

The Maiden can also represent the time when bleeding has just come and is more wild and free. The universal symbol for this spirit is the Waxing Moon.

The Mother

This is at the phase that is (or often is) ovulatory, meaning the time when the womb becomes receptive to sperm and a fertilized egg….also meaning the time you are most open to conceive an idea! The ovulatory phase includes so much work within the body in so little time. All sides and functions of the womb alter for a short period of time to become inhabitable and welcoming to new life.

Likewise a Mother runs around, taking care of every little thing in life--be it children, a business, or a volunteer project. No one really ever sees what goes into the massive effort...and yet what happened every time was nothing short of a miracle. “New life” and “creation” are not here terms limited to child bearing and rearing. In reality, the Womb is capable of offering power, charge, and healing to the entire body, as well as accepting those things into itself.

The Mother is a nurturer and a creatrix--she holds infinite power...she transforms and blossoms, every few weeks simultaneously being caterpillar, cocoon, and butterfly. When there is nothing in sight a mother can create and fix and build.

A Mother knows the importance of prioritizing--realizing who and what they honestly has time for right now. They are intuitive...they take note (physically and mentally) of their menstrual cycle, moods, feelings, activities...they know this of the things they care most surrounding them as well. Mothers gets shit done.

Mothers are represented by pregnancy and fertility, which again do not always necessarily mean an actual living child. The Mother archetype is commonly represented by the Full Moon.

The Enchantress

Represented by those moments leading up to the time you bleed (the Luteal phase), the Enchantress is not always welcome when they unleash personal truths, feelings, and needs upon the world!

The Enchantress, also called a Wild Woman, needs to spend time with themself in reflection, as equally as they need to be out in the world gaining experiences and taking chances.

Enchantresses sometimes forget that they can ask for help, loving, or support. Everyone needs those things and needing them does not make one weak. They also needs to remember that they deserve time alone and away from prying demands.

They are a mentor to all who wish for freedom and happiness...a leader towards what is good and what is best...The Enchantress emerges within when they are needed in even the most humble and meek of people.

A mysterious and powerful entity, The Enchantress is represented by the dark New Moon.

The Crone

Menstrual Blood has often been called the “wise blood”, so it makes sense the final phase is that of the Crone. During this most messy of phases, the body becomes more bloated, receptive to water weight, and in need of extra nourishment and treats. Due to demeaning and patriarchal modern perceptions of these natural occurrences, this phase becomes a self-esteem attack for many.

Slow, yet ever-present, the Crone is a person who simultaneously holds a wealth of well-earned information and also slowly becomes invisible to outsiders through the inevitable loss of youth, fertility, and mobility.

Meditations, connecting with others on similar paths as well as full of wisdom, spending time with and understanding your own self...these actions can all aid you in coming to know yourself on the deeper level you crave. Taking the time to invest in your goals is where many impatient people mess up, but the crone is aware of what Divine Timing can do.

The wise crone knows much, but judges very few. A crone is an individual amongst millions. They willingly let go of that which doesn't serve them, those things which take more than they are willing to give. They are at peace with themself and the world around them, even as they fight for change.

The crone acts more and more as a portal to the Ancestors as each day goes by, channeling others needs as they becomes more in tune with humanity and the family bloodline in general.

Healthy blood flow is easy, bright red color, no clots….the Crone represents this ancient vitality. They are represented as well by those strange years before menopause actually occurs, when symptoms sometimes arise out of the blue and must be dealt with accordingly throughout the transition. This is also relevant to the Crone's symbol the Waning Moon, a symbol often known to represent life and death.

How do you feel about your moon cycle, honestly? Why do you think you feel this way?

The first time you bled, who was there? What happened?

Do you think it is important to celebrate a youth experiencing their first period? What do you think that would change for a child? What do you think it would change for the stigma and attitude around menstruation currently and historically to celebrate and honor this time?

How would you celebrate a young person's first period?

What are some ways that our culture shames and stigmatizes the natural body cycle of menstruation?

What are ways we can change this common and uneducated rhetoric with the next generation?

What are ways we can demand respect from people who may be used to treating menstrual blood as gross, dirty, or unnatural?

What are your unhealthiest menstrual cycle habits? Don't be afraid to be honest with yourself! (Ask: Do you chart your cycle? What do you do when you have cramps--do you even respond? Are you using items you know are probably unhealthy for your vagina and womb (and Nature)? Are you doing anything to heal yourself? etc)

Natural Alternatives to Tampons and Pads

As the days go on, many people are realizing that tampons and pads traditionally bought in stores come with many risks, including the chemicals placed inside of them to give unnatural scent and heightened absorption, as well as the risks of inserting cotton in your vaginal walls. This can lead to Toxic Shock Syndrome (TSS), vaginal irritation, UTIs, cramping, and fibroids, hysterectomy, and even cancer. This doesn't even begin to cover the massive waste and destruction that all these plastic applicators and pads are wrecking on the environment after only one use...part of connecting with our bodies naturally reminds us of our long history of treating the environment with respect too.

Thankfully, there are now alternatives to these unhealthy methods, and many are non intrusive and involve one purchase for years at a time!

- Period Panties: These are probably the easiest transition to make if you are able to invest. You can buy varying panties that can, yes, absorb the blood from your period with nothing other than the panties on! The quality ranges with price, however. For $15-20 on Amazon you can purchase a pair that will last a few hours with normal flow or with a light period (usually to be used in conjunction with a pad or sea sponge, or even cup if you are worried about leaking). For $50+/each you could invest in 3-6 solid pairs that can each last all day or all night with an extremely heavy flow. These underwear are built to last a long time and in fact get more absorbent with each wash.
- Cloth Pads: Another method that requires investment but work similarly to period panties are cloth pads. Some people hand wash, and others simply toss these in the wash. They are always there when you

need one, fold up discreetly to tuck in your bag, and best of all come in just about every design under the sun thanks to the people who make them at home and sell online. An easier investment to make, a set will cost you $30-100, but again this investment lasts you your entire life.

- Menstrual Cup: A simple, no mess solution to periods! Many who use this method could not *imagine* having to go back to free flowing into their pants after using tampons for so long. They know the ultimately healthiest method is non-insertion, but they are professionals, or mobile and active, and really would just prefer to get something simple and reliable, without breaking the bank. The menstrual cup is a solution you could look into for yourself.
  There are many brands of menstrual cups on the market, but all are basically what they sound like-- a little silicone "cup" inserted into the vaginal canal that fills up with menstrual blood and can be emptied in the toilet. These tend to hold decent amounts, allowing even the heaviest cycle to go hours without change. Best of all, it is a one time purchase of $20-80 and can be used for *years* after. This is an excellent way to collect blood for your plants or any rituals or conjure work you may do, such as for Self-Love.
- Menstrual Sponge: The next natural internal choice is the sea sponge. Though they need to be replaced every 5-6 months, they are a very natural and gentle method of absorbing your period blood, and range from around $10-40 per package, depending on size and set. Looking exactly like the bath sponges you see in other beauty sections on the market, their purpose works similarly, absorbing your menstrual blood. Some may find this method more messy, but it is undoubtedly healthy and a perfect alternative to tampon users!
- Cloth Tampon: A cheap option, you still need to be careful of! Though it's extremely rare, cloth tampons *still* put you at risk for TSS (toxic shock syndrome). TSS happens when a tampon is left in far too long--usually days. People choose to leave a tampon in for more than a 8 hours for various personal reasons, but this is not safe. TSS is a bacterial infection with symptoms including fever, vomiting, low blood

pressure, a rash and more. Again, though rare,if any of these symptoms seem to sneak up on you, seek medical care immediately. Cloth tampons can be easily handmade with a small and rolled up absorbent cloth, crochet, knitting, and some people even use a simple rolled baby sock. They can be purchased online as well, with usually four or so being bought every set. These are safer than average tampons because you can choose the fabric and it will not have the chemicals and scents found in store bought versions.

After reading the above list of healthier alternatives for commercial tampons and pads, what are some ways you think seem like something you could put into your menstrual health routine? Specifically focus on making *your* cycle habits more healthy!

Charting Your Cycle

Keeping track of your cycle helps you stay on top of your health and understanding your body. It is one of the most surface level forms of connecting with the womb because it's about what your *senses* are telling you about your body.

One of the most common ways to chart your cycle is by simply making the days you have your period down in a calendar. When I had my first period in the 7th grade, one of the gifts I was bought was a tiny two year calendar to circle the dates in. Remembering what days you are on your cycle helps you establish patterns, notice if something is abnormal, or if everything's the same. This practice will tell you how long your cycle is (usually 27-29 days) and this information is useful not only for your personal knowledge for sexual and lifestyle activities, but also for speaking about your health with your doctor. You will always know when your last period was, and what your symptoms typically are if you are even slightly detailed.

Another common way to track your fertility and menstrual bleeding is to pay close attention to the cervical fluids you see (or don't) each day. Typically after the period, vaginal sensations are drier. With no mucus, the vagina is a toxic place for sperm, killing it within 4 hours. After 2-3 dry days, mucus will start to appear signifying you are fertile. It will progress from pasty, to creamy, to a slippery egg white within days. This mucus is what keeps sperm alive, and it also is happening right as your eggs are getting ready for fertilization. After the vaginal mucus appears like slippery egg white, typically the vaginal sensation dries back up and continues this way until the next period. You can check your mucus by wiping and checking the cloth/toilet paper. You can also wash your hands, insert a finger and gently swipe inside, near the cervix (which usually feels soft and higher in the vagina when you are fertile, and firm and lower in the vagina when you are not).

A final way to track your fertility is by charting your waking temperature. This is your temperature before you even sit up in bed or make love in the morning. Usually your temperature is *cool* before ovulation (due to your eggs making estrogen) and *warm* after ovulation (due to the empty shell that once held your egg producing progesterone). Though the temperature "jump" is a relatively small one, when tracking this on a chart, you can determine if your temperature drops back down (indicating the fertile cycle is ending) or if it remains warmer (indicating pregnancy) This method does require a digital thermometer with memory (preferably a "basal thermometer" for best results). Keeping this thermometer by your bed, take your temperature every morning at the same time, when you wake up (before even going to the bathroom). Some people get a thermometer with an alarm, wake up to take their temperature and then go right back to sleep, charting later using the memory function. Because you can see immediately if your temperature drops back down or not, this method helps you know if you are pregnant (or not) sooner. An excellent resource for learning to track your fertility in further depth (especially with use of waking temperature) is the *Honoring Our Cycles Workbook* by Katie Singer.

Of course, everyone is different. Some people have more discharge than others, and some release mucus during their period. I have several times heard Elders say, "If you really want to have sex, you're fertile," and I like to think that's a good general rule, but please be honest with your own body, vagina, and its cycles and habits.

Charting your cycle today has been made really simple with apps for the phone, tablet, and computer. There are apps that allow you to chart in your basal body temperature to easily see temperature changes, note the stickiness of your cervix mucus, your symptoms, your moon cycle length, and can give increasingly accurate fertility information.

You should never rely on just one method of fertility tracking to ensure you are or are not fertile. If you're not sure if you're fertile or not, and you do not want a child, use protection.

Below I have provided some charts for you to either fill out here, or copy for use elsewhere. Chart as much or as little as you'd like, but commit to begin charting at least *one sign* of your fertility, even if it's only on days of your period. Remember *the only 100% way to avoid pregnancy is to keep your womb away from sperm.*

On the next few pages I have included a chart for you to either fill out here or make multiple copies of for personal use. Some of the spaces are self explanatory, but I will still write how to fill them out here:

- Start/End Dates: This is filled out to give you ease when looking back at your chart later.
- # of Days In Cycle: After the cycle, write how many days from the first day of your period to the day before your next one occurs. This will help you gain an understanding of your typical cycle days, or if yours can even be predicted at all right now.
- Date: Write the actual date to also aid in later referencing.
- Intercourse: This space can help you keep track of any time a penis has been in your vagina *and* keep track of your sexual encounters/partners in general which can also be very useful information down the line for personal and medical use.

- Time Temp Taken: Put the time you always do it *or* only note the times when you do not manage to take it at the usual time (which should be noted at least once on the page for reference.)
- Waking Temperature: This section will look something like, "97.8, 97.3, 97.6, 97.8" and around 15 days into your cycle, switch to being in a little over 98 degrees and read "98.6, 98.7, 98.6, 98.5" etc. This small change of a higher temperature is a reflection of your fertility. After another 10 days or so, there will be a drop in temperature down to the original temperature again, indicating the cycle has passed. If the temperature does not drop, a pregnancy is highly likely.
  Again, this is a more involved process and will require more research to use for birth control purposes, but can be an excellent indicator of pregnancy (allowing you to tell the difference between a heavy period and a miscarriage).
- Mood: Try for one word to describe your overall energy of the day. "Excited", "annoyed", or "calm" are examples.
- Menstrual Cycle: Here, simply mark the days of your period with a small star or check. You can use other symbols to indicate a heavier or lighter flow, or spotting.
- Cervix: Here is where you can note how your cervix feels if you choose to reach your finger to the back of your vagina and feel for it (it feels kind of like a nose tip). Use "F" for a firm, low, and closed feeling cervix. Use "S" for a soft, high, and open feeling cervix.
- Mucus: Daily check your vaginal mucus and note the texture (creamy, sticky, egg white, crumbly etc). If you are dry, note that too. You can also use this section to give more detail about your blood flow during your period if you need to.
- Moon Cycle: Although this term often is used in place of the word "period", here it literally means the lunar phase so that you can compare this to your bleeding cycle more easily. Take the time to draw in the major moon cycles, such as the full and new moon. Include other information to give yourself a more detailed chart.

- Miscellaneous: This section can include exercise you have done that day, what yoni egg you are using, if you did a sacred bath, if you had a headache or cramps, or if you partook in extra sugars. Feel free to make it your own.

Start Date: # Of Days This Cycle:

End Date: Fertility Cycle #:

Cycle Day	1	2	3	4	5	6	7	8	9	10	11	12	13	14	15	16	17	18	19	20	21	22	23	24	25	26	27	28	29	30	31	32	33	34	35	36	37	38	39	40	41
Date																																									
Intercourse																																									
Time Temp Taken																																									
Waking Temp																																									
Mood																																									
Menstrual Cycle																																									
Cervix																																									
Mucus																																									
Moon Cycle																																									
Miscellaneous																																									

Womb Healing Workbook I

Start Date: # Of Days This Cycle:

End Date: Fertility Cycle #:

Cycle Day	1	2	3	4	5	6	7	8	9	10	11	12	13	14	15	16	17	18	19	20	21	22	23	24	25	26	27	28	29	30	31	32	33	34	35	36	37	38	39	40	41
Date																																									
Intercourse																																									
Time Temp Taken																																									
Waking Temp																																									
Mood																																									
Menstrual Cycle																																									
Cervix																																									
Mucus																																									
Moon Cycle																																									
Miscellaneous																																									

Womb Healing Workbook I

Start Date: # Of Days This Cycle:

End Date: Fertility Cycle #:

Cycle Day	1	2	3	4	5	6	7	8	9	10	11	12	13	14	15	16	17	18	19	20	21	22	23	24	25	26	27	28	29	30	31	32	33	34	35	36	37	38	39	40	41
Date																																									
Intercourse																																									
Time Temp Taken																																									
Waking Temp																																									
Mood																																									
Menstrual Cycle																																									
Cervix																																									
Mucus																																									
Moon Cycle																																									
Miscellaneous																																									

Womb Healing Workbook I

Start Date: # Of Days This Cycle:

End Date: Fertility Cycle #:

Cycle Day	1	2	3	4	5	6	7	8	9	10	11	12	13	14	15	16	17	18	19	20	21	22	23	24	25	26	27	28	29	30	31	32	33	34	35	36	37	38	39	40	41
Date																																									
Intercourse																																									
Time Temp Taken																																									
Waking Temp																																									
Mood																																									
Menstrual Cycle																																									
Cervix																																									
Mucus																																									
Moon Cycle																																									
Miscellaneous																																									

Abuse

******This section is for sexual and physical abuse.*

The womb holds on to *all* of our memories--the good and the bad. Trauma from abuse changes the way we look at ourselves and the world. As you come to love yourself and your body more and more, you will also come to release the pain and trauma that you have been carrying, even as you never forget what happened to you.

This Workbook does not address abuse in full detail, because the next two Womb Healing Workbooks (2: Overcoming Sexual Abuse, and 3: Overcoming Childhood Sexual Abuse) are for this purpose, as I think these subjects need more than just a couple of pages to delve into and recover from...however I do still think we need to address your pain and recovery.

Using the picture shown next, label from head to toe what parts of your body have been abused, who did it, and how old you were:

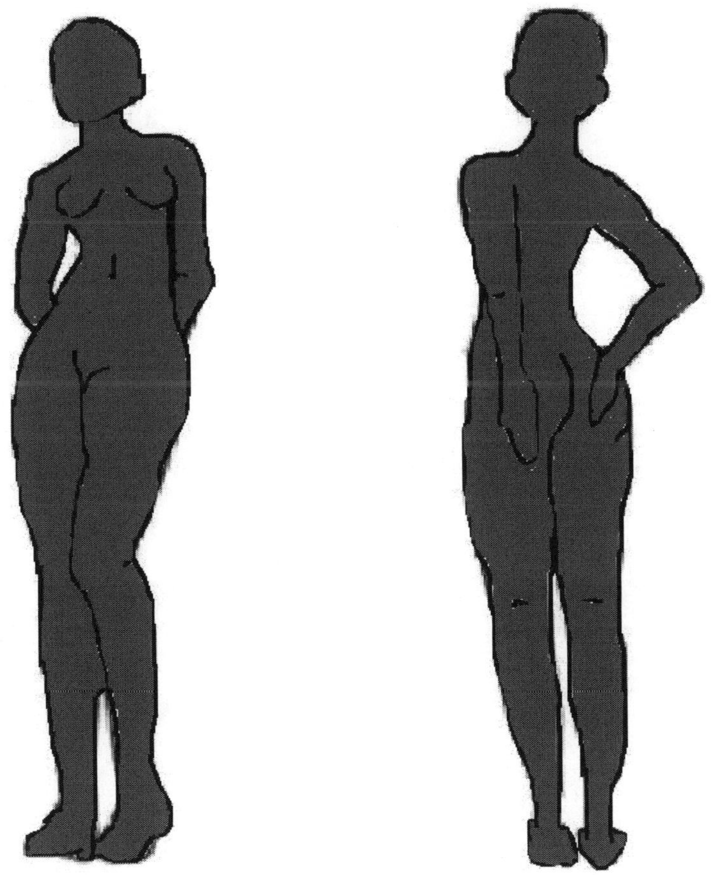

Who would you be, had you never been abused?

What would you *not* be today that you cherish, had you never been abused?

What happened to your abuser?

What would you do to your abuser if there were no punishments?

What can you do to punish abusers in the future? What can be done to make abusers feel unsafe, as you once did?

What would it take for you to heal from this abuse? How can you make this happen?

Pussy Prayer

Pussy prayer is less about sex and more about what we *use* for sex. passion, energy, creativity, and life. Pussy prayer is a way to honor onh lo lle of human beings' closest ways to the Ether—where before life and afterlife rest. Pussy is a portal to God. As we worship the Creator, we worship where the Creator sends creations through.

Whether you are horny, emotional, or orgasming….it's all energy! Utilize that energy by connecting it to Work you are doing.Allow your sexuality to become a source of power for you as you focus on your journey of growth.

When you decide to use your punani for manifestation and prayer, be specific. Have a real goal in mind, write it down, and focus only on the pleasure of your success. Don't be vague or add too many subjects to each session. Spread them out and cherish your decision to pour your energy into this future.

Below, fill out the chart with your own manifestations, the sexual energy you put towards it, and check back every 6 months to a year and see your progress in your goals.

Date:	Manifestation:	Notes:	Update:

Part Three: Matrilineal Meditations

Honey Pot Chronicles #3

I sat up when I realized
I wasn't home.
The wind blew warm against my skin and I
sat in the humid depths of a world I did not know.
My heart beat steady on my ribs and
in my ears.
I thought at first I was frightened, but soon
I realized I was not alone...

I was not alone. I was not alone.
The beat wasn't my heart
It was the drums
And though I usually overthink,
I did not have to pause in the moment--
I moved,
I prayed,
I praised,
I breathed,
I followed.

In my calm came my answer
when through the dew and leaves I stepped and
Every toe rested within the sand.

***You have returned*, they told me.**
& each took their turn to look deep in my eyes
& remind me of my bloodline.
Shells in my hair,
paint on my skin
The bright of the moon ruled us
Tradition -- centuries old
I have returned...
I have returned...

Matrilineal Descent

The connection to our matrilineal Ancestors is such a deep and special one. Consider: Before you were born, you sat as an egg within a womb yourself and within weeks of fertilization also had a womb with all of the eggs you would ever carry! And so this special connection is held by all those with wombs, an experience unlike any other.

The womb (and your blood and your DNA) all hold on to things! Good and bad, it can all be retained and passed down generationally, either physically, spiritually, or emotionally. It is no surprise then to hear that scientists are finding patterns between traumas that happened 100 years ago, and peoples lifestyle and attitudes today.

Black people everywhere are trying to let go of their past traumas, break the cycle, and reclaim our power. This cannot be done without fully learning and addressing what happened to you and to your family. This cannot be done without being a healer, in every sense of the word. Healing generational trauma is not an easy feat, and will most likely take several lifetimes to complete. Every time you think you are done, you aren't...and that doesn't mean you are failing at all. It may be frustrating, but only because you are not aware of the bigger picture.

To begin connecting with your Ancestors, you should speak with them and honor them. You should already have a simple altar dedicated to your Ancestors...it can be as simple as a glass of water and an ankh, and as dressed up as you like, including pictures, flower, food, and more, depending on your space and preference. The better you *can* make your altar look, the better it *should* look, *but* that doesn't always translate to more items, so make sure that your altar is somewhere you find beautiful, meaningful and enjoyable to sit by.

Make a corner of your altar dedicated to your matrilineal side--all of the work. womb bearers, the feminine people that were related to and raised yourself and those closest to you. Make time to talk with, remember, and build relationships with them. Remember that these are the Ancestors you call for certain needs...to rectify certain offenses. Knowing the right time to call on these Ancestors (and when to call on others) takes intuition, but is an invaluable skill.

Do not feel the need to call to every which Ancestor. Be frugal. Tell abusers, and greedy or cruel to leave. Do not call on anyone who hurt you or who you believe the worst about (or who believed the worst about you). Watch out for ones whose core beliefs went fundamentally against your own. Not all Ancestors need to be deeply involved in your spiritual practice--or even involved at all! Be as moral, wise, and intuitive as you can during this process...after all this is about your spiritual health and well being, as well as your loved ones.

Name Ancestors you wish to build relationships with:

Prayer

Daily

Make time to say "Thank You" daily. Make time to immerse yourself in gratitude and spirit, make time to call to the Ancestors to talk (and don't forget to also make time to listen!) Commit yourself to some kind of ritual that works for you and do it every day to the best of your abilities. Prayer not only lets your Ancestors know you are grateful, but that you fully intend to act and walk in ways beneficial for your bloodline (and therefore them) as well.

Your small daily ritual does not have to be kneeling by the bedside as one often imagines when they think of prayers. Call upon your bloodline for ideas! Consider, for example, the *sangomas* (traditional healers) of South Africa, who every morning pray to their Ancestors by burning a sacred plant that nourishes the spirits of their old ones.

Cut fruit to offer daily that you change every morning. Dance. Ring a bell. Speak aloud 10 things you are grateful for. Sing a special song that you cherish in your heart. Recite a powerful poem. Anoint a statue with oils. Use prayer beads. The options for showing your respect are endless, as long as your focus is on your Ancestors and prayer.

Your daily prayer is less of a time to ask for things, and more of a time to feel the joy and greatness of what already is. Insert your own character and *ashe* into your spiritual Work.

Remember to not only speak from the heart, but to speak with conviction. You have the authority to speak to your Ancestors, so talk and ask. It becomes easier with practice and time to give a powerful prayer such as those that Elders and the Initiated have been seen to give.

General Prayer

*I call to my Ancestors, both known and unknown. (*Name any Ancestors by name you would like to). *Blessings and gratitude to you for your presence and influence in my life. I love and miss you presence here on Earth but gather strength and wisdom from your continued energy and guidance. May your guidance and wisdom continue to be a path opener for me and mine, and may you be with me at every crossroads. May love and prosperity be brought into my home. Ashe.*

Mealtime

Feel blessed for the food that you have the privilege to eat, and the fresh water you have to drink! Feel blessed for your "pot belly"/ "food baby", your curves and rolls and weight. Feel blessed for your muscles, any flat parts, any part you wish was bigger or smaller…feel blessed for your ability to move, and most importantly, your ability to try harder tomorrow at *something.* Expressing your gratitude changes not only the way your mind perceives your food, but the very molecules of the food itself (shown easily in images from the Fujiwara Dam water experiment with prayer).

When praying, it is best to pray from the heart, however it can feel awkward or strange to pray out loud to the Ancestors when we haven't seen many public (or even private) displays of this act.

We do know that it is vital we infuse our Ancestors into our daily life and that includes asking them to bless and revitalize that which gives us energy, health, and wellness...as well as pleasure. In this piece I have compiled a list of ideas to help facilitate the fusion of the Ancestors with our eating habits.

Mealtime Prayer:

Beloved Ancestors,

This home is always open to you as well as our hearts.
We are grateful for all that we have.
We take this time right now
To thank you for our food.

Hetepu.

How To Build a Personal Prayer/Blessing:

- Say a greeting
- Thank the Ancestors for what you are grateful for
- Offer sincere praise at their work in your life
- Share your needs
- Use a formal closing such as "Ashe" (make things happen/ produce change), "Hekau" (words of power), "Hetepu" (peace, contentment, joy, satisfied) or "Ayibobo" (Amen/Hallelujah).

Offerings

One or more times a month, and especially when you make an excellent meal put aside time to place food at the altar say:

"I offer you a share of this meal
that was created with my own hands.

Ancestors, please accept this gift
and throughout my life leave your blessings."

Be sure to regularly feed them something your Ancestors would have traditionally eaten and enjoyed. This may mean learning to cook something you can't stand or refuse to eat! Don't expect your great uncle to respond to tofu if he loved prime rib, and certainly don't starve the Ancestors, especially if the situation requires a real response. There's a line where you are not just being frugal, modern, or innovative, and are just being disrespectful.

Offerings shouldn't be store bought or continuously made by someone else...you putting effort, time, and money into the making of a meal personally is a large part of where the respect comes from.

When you are on your period (or right before it starts!) and you are especially craving something delicious, you can use the opportunity to connect deeper with your mother's mothers. Learn how to bake something scrumptious, perhaps a treasured family recipe, or one with your own twist, and don't forget to cut them a slice and pray with them.

Simple Blessings

Blessings are found in many cultures. There are people who never leave their grandparents or parents home without receiving one. Sometimes they are perfect to pass from a friend to a friend. Others, they are whispered into an ear, or related over the phone. Blessings can jump out from speeches, words, and prayers and the phrase remains in your psyche and continues to fuel you.

Whatever context you find them, blessings can add warmth and ashe to even the coldest and saddest of situations. They give you the "right thing to say" when there's wisdom to be said concisely. And unlike a Romantic Comedy, make it make sense when you give solicited wisdom, if you give it at all.

Next, I have put some of my own, some from Ancestors in history, and some that are common to the world. Adopt them and tweak them to fit your purpose.

- *May the Ancestors bless you.*
- *Walk tall, walk well, walk safe, walk free.* - Xhosa/Zulu Blessing
- *Bless those who bless you, and curse those who curse you.*
- *May your spirit prosper in the Ancestor's care.*

- *Listen to the wind, it talks. Listen to the silence, it speaks. Listen to your heart, it knows.* - Turtle Island Proverb
- *If we are bold, love strikes away the chains of fear from our souls.* - Maya Angelou
- *Through you, our family is blessed.*
- *(You are) deliberate and afraid of nothing.* - Audre Lorde
- *May the Ancestors bless you, keep you, and protect you.*
- *May you know you are blessed, cherished, and carried.*
- *What dreams we have and how they fly.* - Paul Laurence Dunbar
- *May your Ancestors be with you at every crossroads.*
- *You must never be fearful of what you are doing if it is right* - Rosa Parks
- *May you know you are secure in the Ancestor's love.*
- *Hold on to what is good, even if it is a handful of earth.* - Pueblo Prayer
- *You have within you the strength, the patience and the passion to reach for the stars to change the world.* - Harriet Tubman
- *Where there is love, there is no darkness.* - Burundi Blessing
- *May hope overcome your sadness and may joy return.*
- *Thrice happy are they whose love grows stronger day by day* - African American Blessing
- *Don't ever be afraid to come to me n cry...Don't ever hesitate to look me n the eye. Don't ever be afraid to tell me how you feel. Remember you're my girl n we gotta keep it real.* - Nikki Giovanni
- *May the Ancestors come to meet you.*
- *May your soul smile again.*
- *May you have the blessing of being consoled.*

Prayer for Bad Times

I call on the Ancestors because I cannot find hope. I need your strength to face today's hard and troubled times. Enlighten me with the truth, and empower my life with blessings. I invite you into my weakness to create strength--Come before and after me as I walk through the day. I fear nothing with you at my side. Show me the way.

Blessings/Prayers for Child

Don't forget to include children in your prayers and blessings! Benevolent love of children ensures that a world of future peace is possible. Bless children to allow them to walk in the comfort of protection and power. Add something personal if you can, whispered in their ear when you are done. Saying "I love you", or acknowledging or honoring their accomplishments or place in your life allows them to be more receptive to the more personalized blessing.

- *Ancestors, give constant protection and grant a healthy birth.*
- *Let the Ancestors be with you and give you peace.*
- *Ancestors, guard and protect them.*
- *Bless this child's room and keep them in your sight.*
- *May the Ancestors keep you safe.*
- *May you have a long and healthy life.*
- *I speak Ancestral blessings over you.*
- *May your eyes look ahead towards the future.*
- *May you always prosper and be in good health.*

Write your own prayers from the heart below:

Mother Earth

When I try to talk to people about the Earth they are either totally all in to fight for their birthright or totally couldn't give two fucks about the situation because they have bigger things to focus on. I understand all attitudes completely.

The thing is, in these modern times everybody, but most *especially* people of color and even more specifically Black people have been systematically separated from the land they are on. This began with the removal of people from Africa to the Americas and Europe, but it was also seen in predatory sharecropping contracts and attacks on affluent Black people and communities, and then again seen in modern cities in the United States, where redlining is occurs, Black people struggle to gain loans to buy houses, and are foreclosed upon and incarcerated at higher rates than anyone else, leading to a struggle to gain wealth while being trapped in the cities generationally.

With the combination these decades in the cities and the stress of day to day racism from other races who live there, a complete disconnect from the land has occurred. This is further exacerbated by the racist stereotypes of Black people living outside and being "uncivilized", causing many to try and live as the opposite of this trope.

Understanding all this, is it little wonder that many do not see or care what is happening to our planet? Yet all around us Mother Earth screams for attention and love, urging us to make a change towards her improvement and wellbeing. One person cannot change the world, but unless it's your job to rally the world, the only person you should be focused on is *you* anyway… well, you and any children you have committed to raising with your influence!

Our Ancestors loved the Earth, they listened to it. In West Africa, the Ashanti people call the Earth Goddess of fertility Asase Yaa, and her temple is traditionally the actual agricultural fields on which crops are grown. Even when taken to the Americas the tradition of learning and listening to the trees has continued, the tradition of honoring the plant and even material items remained for a long while. There was no overuse or waste--we all have a great-grandma who never wasted a thing.

Choices *not* to overuse and *not* to waste may seem petty and irrelevant. It is not. Just as with all parts of your spiritual practice, the reward is in the Work. Choosing to do things and look at them differently than you did before.

Looking at how many plastic bags you use for sandwiches, produce at the store, and other storage alone is probably mind boggling when you start thinking of the logistics. What are ways you can cut most out from your daily and weekly use? Can you use cloth sandwich bags and toss them in the washer? Can you cut out single-use straws? Is it possible to bring your own bags to the store? What exactly is wrong with picking up trash that you see outside?

Remember that when you are doing these things that preserve the Earth and clean up what is your and your descendants birthright, you are not enabling litterbugs or being used! You are cleaning the Earth, you are influencing others to do better, you are normalizing the caretaking of the Earth as a human practice, you are honoring your Ancestors and their traditional ways, *you are making a change*!

Caring about Mother Earth's physical wellness still difficult for you? I urge you to start connecting with her spiritually anyway. When you connect spiritually, the urge to connect physically naturally comes.

Find a place nearby to go on weekly walks--come to learn and know a tree there. Place offerings and make small offerings around the cities and in trees. Bless the place and leave it better than you found it--make that your motto wherever you go. Write love letters, go sit quietly and meditate somewhere, practice Fire Breathing outside, give yourself a chance to build your lungs somewhere alone. Sing to the Greatest of Mothers, hold a hand to the earth and connect.

Take off your shoes when you are out and about sometimes. Never wear shoes again if you feel like it, it's not actually illegal contrary to popular belief (though you should follow store signs, always). Walk and dance in grass, sand, dirt and pavement. Feel the difference!

Problems/ Ways I Lack Connection with The Earth:	Solutions/ Ways to Connect With the Earth:

Sacred Circle

Creating a space where womb bearers and women can come together is an ancient and necessary tradition. We consecrate this space for the healing and vitality of our wombs and our communities.

After setting up the boundaries which keep you comfortable and able to facilitate a safe and healing space for all, try to open your Sacred Circle up to others!

Before you begin, assign a host to lead the event. This person can change every time, but it should be clear who is leading for everyone to support and the event to run smoothly with the least confusion. When people take turns, it also gives the opportunity to learn from each person and their unique knowledge

Sister Circle General Schedule:

- Dance or smoke cleanse to clear the space and energy around
- Pour libations and pray to the Ancestors/Spirit Guides/Deity(s)
- Introductions of members
- Introduction of topic
- Read from sacred or treasured texts by peers, elders, and Ancestors.
- Group movement (dance, yoga/stretching, seated with upper body only)
- Group activity (ritual, conjure, art, lesson, guest, etc)
- Dance/Potluck
- Closing ceremony/prayer

Ideas/Notes:

Goddess Dancing

The womb requires movement to keep health because of where it's situated underneath the colon and its tendency to float in the space that it has within your body it requires the movement to stretch. When the colon is light, the womb can float, but when it is full of meat and dairy, it can cause constipation, which movement can help relieve.

The only rule or requirement for womb dancing is to lose all inhibition. In order to do this, you must set yourself up for success, creating the environment that will lead to you ultimately connecting further with yourself in the way that you hope to.

If this means that you never dance a day in front of somebody else, that's just fine, but you deserve to spend this time getting to know your body getting to know your own movements how your own muscles work and thrive and how your own body really expresses itself when given the opportunity to just be. Eventually, you can work on finding others to dance or witness with you if you feel inclined.

Goddess dancing is a type of exercise meant to connect you to your body and how it moves, remind you of your inner and outer power, and have you really spend time with your womb space. Try it in different costumes-- from complete nudity to your favorite clothes, or ritual clothes.

Mirror's should only be used if you are at a stage where you think a mirror could help, but it's not about watching yourself, it's about feeling yourself, it's about getting to know your own body and your own movements and trusting them. Don't let yourself get self conscious, and if the mirror is causing this, put it away and don't use anything for a while. Use a phone to record yourself if you are truly curious for a look.

The thing that most of us really look for when we look at a dancer, is that ability to truly connect with and trust your own body to think a movement and translate it with this body and most of us actually spend time the opposite. Being betrayed by our own bodies.

In this exercise, we rewrite that narrative and take that time to really explore our body, much in the way a child explores their body. With no concern for others, thoughts, they bend, jump, roll, eb, and flow.

Allow music to inspire you. Don't choose something just because others might like it, or it might make you more interesting--genuinely choose what you like! No matter the genre or the music choice, allow grace to reside within each step. It doesn't have to be perfect. It will get better every time, as with all things these takes practice and practice is a *must*--there has to be a willingness to put in work.

Physically your womb wants to be free to float within your core...to do this it must be in alignment with your body's digestive system and your movements help facilitate this healthfulness in that area, it strengthens your core. It helps your posture. As you come to understand and connect with your physical body, this confidence and muscle memory will translates to the way you act in everyday life when you aren't dancing. You will begin to trust and depend on your body more and more to do what you have asked of it, the more effort you put into your spiritual movement.

Dancing goes beyond physical and spiritual benefits, and helps emotionally as well. There is no way to feel the movements rolling out of you and not appreciate the strength and resilience from which it comes. Spend time with yourself with your womb feeling, sexy and uplifting to your soul. Exalt the power that your punani and the body it is attached to hold.

It is possible to activate the power within your punani through your movement through smooth, slippery, seductive movements. There is a grace to even the wildest of orgasms, a grace in every clitoris and labia in the way it responds to stimulation. In an enactment of wild and heavy power can be all it takes to release. Begin the journey of true connection between body and your own inner power.

As your new body moves, allow each curve to shake erotically and invitingly. There is a lithe grace to feminine movement that is not determined by size or sex but rather by a complete soul understanding of one's own body and the way it can connect to the divine feminine.

Allow yourself to create womb prayer through your movement.

Body Adornment

There is no one way the Goddess dresses, but there are a few simple guidelines that help when deciding how to shape your wardrobe. If you aren't careful, you can find yourself spending a ton of money on little things that initially excited you, but were quickly forgotten or obsolete and have fallen into the depths of your drawers/closet. Eventually you give away these barely worn and now totally uninspiring clothes to the Goodwill, who tries to sell a fraction of it, and gives the rest for free to poorer countries….these people also can't find as much use for these clothes and they end up wasted and polluting the Earth.

Well *that's* not okay, because didn't we just talk about Mother Earth and how we are going to be more respectful and wiser with our choices surrounding the planet? Thankfully, a wasteful closet can be easily avoided if you pay attention to it.

<u>Tips:</u>

- Do not purchase items you don't totally love. Seriously. Don't buy things because it's in style or whatever, buy it because wearing it gives you pure joy in your soul, because it makes you feel *good*, because it sets your emotions on fire and gives you confidence for the day! Items are not just about how much they cost per wear, but how much joy they give you every time you wear them!
- Get rid of excess! Reduce the amount of clothes that are in your closet, starting with items you have never worn and you have no emotional attachment to. Toss things that haven't fit or been used in years. Donate anything that you barely remembered you had or that you were gifted and you never really liked. If you wouldn't wear it today, get rid of it. Release.
- Dress not for what you *could* be or what others are wearing but what really looks good on you and who you are *now*. Only spend money on items and in stores that fit you really well, especially once you've found which stores those are! Research your body type and experiment with different styles.
- Do *not* buy ill fitting clothes just because they are cheap! Only buy things you need or that will give you joy. Buying things just because they are cheap is how these items build up and clutter your home.
- Have a goal in mind. If you have a set look, of course you should have alternative outfits and ways to present yourself, but overall you should have a defined "look" that can be easily added to over the years. With a few essentials that can be used for all of your favorite looks, you can set yourself up for success.
- Try saving for the essentials. Obviously you can't always wait until you've tucked away $100+ to get the perfect item, but investing does have its perks! When you buy high quality essential items (denim jeans, black pants, a dress, a winter coat) you know that your wardrobe will have staples to build off of for years to come. These items tend to last longer than the cheaper alternatives, have thicker fabric so they don't require layering and look more expensive, and also tend to fit better as well.

- Try to focus on having 9 bottoms, 9 tops, and five pairs of shoes for everyday use, especially if you are someone who has way too many articles of clothing and are wasteful when it comes to clothing. Allow these items to take you over a decent range of activities you do daily, such as work, errands/activities, daily life, dressed up, and fun times.
- Next focus on the items you need that are not day to day. Loungewear, swimwear/workout, outerwear, and formalwear (including accessories). You should also have some items like t-shirts and tanks for layering.
- Make sure you don't mistake trends for investments! Most trends aren't timeless.
- Be patient for sales. Often clothes are overpriced...if you can be patient for the right
- If you want to wear makeup well, practice. If you need to look immaculate, hire a professional makeup artist.
- Piercings and tattoos are traditional indigenous body art. They often can be symbolic and meaningful, however today are associated negatively when seen on brown skin. Find a tattoo artist who is able to work with your skin tone and achieve what you want. All of your body adornments should be done by someone whose energy you do not mind transfering to yourself.

Waistbeads

One of my favorite expressions of femininity is waistbeads. Waistbeads are a traditional practice in many parts of Africa that is done just like it sounds--tying a string of beads around your waist.

Traditionally worn to show weight gain, tribe, status, fertility, and more, waistbeads are worn by black people in the diaspora as a representation of black pride, the divine feminine, and to track waist size.

Waistbeads can be purchased or made and used to keep track of or celebrate anything you can think of. As a reward for completing this journey, I highly encourage gifting yourself with a new set to grace your hips.

Write about your ideal wardrobe:

Book of Power

A "Book of Power" also called a Grimoire or Spellbook is a notebook, journal, document, or binder in which one writes down their spiritual and magical journey. From roots they have worked, to conjure methods used, to places they have visited and practices they have tried, people of all practices find it beneficial to have this special book. There are *so* many important reasons to write down your journey.

First and foremost--you are taking care of your health. Tracking which herbs you have been using or recently introduced to your own body can help figure out what works and doesn't work, as well as what you may have a bad reaction to.

The same concept goes beyond your physical wellness to your spiritual and emotional wellness. When you write down the steps you have taken you can find what cures and helps heal certain trauma and grief that you have suffered in *your own way*. You can find what herbs your womb really likes when you take note of what is in the teas you blend. You can remember exactly which time you had the breakthrough in your meditation, or a unique experience at the altar. Even if you're not "one of those people", it is always a rewarding experience to go back and read previous thoughts and words.

It is helpful to have a written (and visual if you use drawings or polaroids) reminder of your spiritual workings and efforts. Replicating them later or remember specific sequences all are easier when you can remember exactly what it was you did. Sharing the information with whoever teaches you, or even with those you teach is also easier in this format. Passing on your information is also available to give to future generations in your family, even with death or suppression, when the words are written down. It gives just one more chance for your truth and customs to continue passing down through the generations.

Plan out your Book of Power below:

Castor Oil Pack

The castor oil pack is a traditional womb healing method of soaking a cloth in castor oil, and applying it to the womb area. The castor oil soaks out toxins, promoting both cleansing as well as blood circulation. Castor oil packs also stimulate the lymphatic system, and liver function.

Use of a castor oil pack is both spiritual and physical. If you are having cramps, a castor oil pack can help remove the symptoms. Similarly, if your womb feels empty or void, or has suffered recent trauma, a castor oil pack can help cleanse and relieve symptoms as well.

The womb is around 4 finger widths below your navel. When using a castor oil pack, be sure to wear clothes that you do not mind getting dirty. Leave the pack on for 45-80 minutes, keeping your body relaxed and rested.

After you remove the pack, feel free to give yourself a gentle massage. Do not try to move your womb around as an expert would... rather take this moment as an opportunity to connect with your womb, see how this space is doing and come to know the energy and symptoms better than you have before.

Even though you are gentle, do not be afraid to add pressure to your womb. This is your body. Come to know it. Do your best to keep the experience feeling good and positive. If you intuitively feel you need to take this further, consider hiring a traditional womb massager to spend time checking and aligning your womb.

There is a power to touching your own womb, and using your own hands to heal. Beyond that, it is an intimate process, coming to know your womb from the outside in this way. Especially during times of womb pain, overcome shyness and get to know your body and listen to what your womb is saying that it needs.

Consider using the Castor Oil Pack not only when you are actively feeling womb pain (physically or emotionally). Try to have Castor Oil handy to use as a healing ritual before sacred Goddess Baths, womb meditation, or even prior to ritual.

Reflection and Notes:

Womb Sauna

Also commonly referred to as a "vaginal steam" "v-steam" or a "yoni steam" in popular culture, the womb sauna is another ancient practice that has been adapted and become utilized by modern womb bearers worldwide. Many accuse this of being a new fad, but the use of steam and smoke to cleanse the womb and body are practices found worldwide in indigenous cultures from The Americas through Africa and up into Asia.

A womb sauna can be done wet *or* dry, just like a regular body sauna! They are typically practiced after childbirth (wait a few weeks after c-section), child loss (miscarriage, abortion, stillbirth), trauma, *or* as a means to promote fertility or womb health. This is a useful practice on both sides of menopause, and are also healing after hysterectomy or myomectomy. Always be sure you are *not* bleeding from your womb when using a womb sauna.

Those who suffer a cold womb will also find these methods of use. Spending time on the womb sauna is an excellent way to reconnect with your womb center, especially if you've been feeling disconnected lately. Worldwide saunas are used to release impurities physically *and* spiritually, and reclaiming this tradition with your womb is a powerful step towards new goals and beginnings.

A *wet womb sauna* is the process of allowing steaming, herbal water to rise and steam your vulva and vaginal canal as you sit over it. Usually, a wooden box is used as a chair, with a hole cut in the seat, though people often make their own alternatives to use (I have a simple one pictured on the following page). A thick blanket is typically wrapped around the body from the belly down to prevent the escape of steam and make the process warm and comfortable, but is not necessary especially on hot days or for bodies that need air to heal. Lighter blankets or sheets can be used instead.

Though there is little agreement about where the wet womb steam originated, the most ancient sources found are in Central and South America, though Korea and Greece have their own traditional versions. Regardless of where it began, this practice has been adopted worldwide by people with a womb to steam, and spas now can be found that offer them for general treatment. Considered a way to improve womb vitality, the wet steam is a way to soften and release buildup in the vaginal canal, as well as nourish it. This is specifically done not only through the steam, but in the specific herbs used for the water the steam rises from. and a wet womb steam can be found to nourish a dry uterus.

A *dry womb sauna* is the process of rubbing the body down in oils, then allowing smoke from burning herbs and/or wood to rise and bath your entire body in smoke as you sit over it. Again a blanket is wrapped around the body from the neck down and you sit over the herbs, perhaps in a clay pot buried in the earth, or a box with a hole. This sauna is sat on until the heat becomes too much.

Incense and herbal smoke bathing dates back to the ancient northeast African kingdoms of Meroe and Nubia. A prominent example of this is the *Dukhan*, a traditional medicine technique found in Sudan, typically given to womb bearers in preparation for marriage, during marriage, and after childbirth. The Dukhan is said to be relaxing, smooths the skin, narrows the vagina, and can even treat syphilis, gonorrhoea and rheumatic pain. The practice leaves a pleasant scent and slight skin coloring, due to the acacia used (and in fact Dukhan creams are purchasable which will give the orange tint to the skin for those who can't do the traditional method).

For many, this simple practice is enough to regulate irregular cycles, fix imbalances. Others experience a reduction in menstrual pain and a release in old blood as their womb relaxes. When the heat of the Womb Sauna reaches the womb tissues, circulation is encouraged. As the blood flow increases and the muscle relaxes, fertility is supported. Postpartum, it helps release fluids and allow the body and stomach to shrink down. Pain during intercourse can also be relieved through this healing method, and some have spoken of using the womb sauna as prolapse prevention.

The other benefit of this is time spent on yourself and with your womb. Having the opportunity to just *fully relax* on a seat, (with a good book, or a meditation or music playing) for 10-30 minutes is healing and rejuvenating in itself, and gives you time to really assess your wellness. You should not steam while on your period or still bleeding/open after childbirth/loss, as steaming speeds up blood flow and could cause heavy bleeding.

What a womb sauna is not going to do is clean your vagina...the vagina is able to clean itself on its own! Heat is medicine for the womb, a way to allow the large muscle relax and rejuvenate itself, thus aiding in the releases that already occur within the womb naturally.

Warning:

- Look up *all herbs* before use! You never know which one might work against a condition you have, or have a side effect that you cannot handle right now.
- Leave the steam if you get a hot flash or it becomes unbearable!
- Do not steam after conception--even possible conception! Steaming could affect the sperm negatively and could even negatively affect implantation.

Set Up

Purchasing a premade wooden box with a hole on top, or an electric steamer can cost $200-500. Making your own is time consuming and just another skill to learn if you don't know how to work with wood already.

If you need to make a womb sauna *in minutes*, I would suggest a hardy cardboard box on a crate as a temporary solution. Cut a hole in the box, flip it over, and place on a milk crate or similar. The bowl of burning or boiling herbs can be placed inside of this, and you can sit over the box.

A more permanent solution is pictured here. Using a folding camping/sports chair (the cloth ones that many of us have in storage, garages, or closets), cut a small hole in the seat of this (not too big! You can always make it bigger), and simply placing the pot of herbs below this. I think this is the most ideal solution as it caters to the greatest range of weights/sizes, is fairly comfortable to sit on, and can be made cheaply (potentially for nothing if you already have an extra one). Further, you can use this chair outside, in the living room, anywhere you need! The perfect portable solution for people who use womb saunas at home as well as professionally.

<u>Wet Womb Sauna Tools</u>:

- 15 - 30 minutes.
- Clay, Glass, Ceramic, or Steel pot (avoid plastic and remember glass is prone to breaking if the water is too hot so remain cautious).
- Smaller bowl within (for easier cleanup)
- 1-2 Cups of Herbs (suggestions below)
- Approximately a half gallon of water
- Large blanket

- Spiritual book, healing prayers, mantra, journal, etc, for use while steaming
- Chair with hole in the seat
- Timer

Optional:

- Light Candles
- Diffuse Essential Oils
- Light Incense
- Play Music

Wet Womb Sauna Herb Recommendations:

- Rose petal
- Yarrow
- Hibiscus
- Raspberry Leaf
- Lavender
- Calendula
- Thyme
- Motherwort
- Burdock
- Lemon Grass
- Basil
- Passion fruit
- Rosemary
- Orange Peel
- Chamomile
- Jasmine
- Dandelion
- Morinda
- Cinnamon Sticks
- Oregano
- Yellow Dock

Directions:

- Take herbs and mix with around a gallon of water. Bring to a rolling boil.
- Place bowl inside of the pot.
- Pour heated water into the bowl
- Cover the pot with the chair, and sit down.
- Wrap the blanket around the waist to trap in more steam and heat.
- Time for 15 minutes. Do whatever relaxing or spiritual work you would prefer in this time.
- When the time is up, remove the blanket and go lay down and relax for another 10-15 minutes afterwards, or longer as needed for healing.
- Consider placing oils by your side to do a womb/vulva massage after.

Dry Womb Sauna Tools:

- 15 - 30 minutes.
- Medium sized incense bowl
- 1-2 Cups of Herbs (suggestions below)
- Incense coals and Lighter/Matches
- Large blanket
- Spiritual book, healing prayers, mantra, journal, etc, for use while steaming
- Chair with hole in the seat
- Timer

Optional:

- Light Candles
- Diffuse Essential Oils
- Burn Incense
- Play Music

Dry Womb Sauna Herb Recommendations:

- Sandalwood
- Acacia (Talh)
- Frankincense

- Myrrh
- Sage
- Cedar
- Sweetgrass
- Copal
- Lavender
- Red Willow Bark

Directions:
- Light the coals and put them inside of a fire safe bowl.
- Place the bowl inside of the pot.
- Pour the dry herbs on top of the lit coals.
- Cover the pot with the chair, and sit down.
- Wrap the blanket around the body from the neck down to trap in more smoke and heat.
- Start for 5-10 min and work your way up to 20. You will most likely sweat from the heat. **Get up and leave if you feel lightheaded or overheated.**
- Do whatever relaxing or spiritual thinking you would prefer in this time.
- Rub and massage your body down with oils, spending special time on your womb, then relax for another 10-15 minutes afterwards, or longer as needed for healing.

The longer you do either of these practices, the longer you will find you are able to do each womb sauna session for.
Talk with your doctor about saunas and if it is safe for you to use them.

Notes:

7 Day Punani Candle

Copy or trace one of the symbols or pictures below onto a paper and tape or glue it to your 7-day candle.

You can use a Punani centered candle for anything punani related...from your own sexual exploration and discovery, to your sex life and relationships, and even to stop or start certain feelings that you might be having.

Redraw and color the punani drawings, write names, utilize symbols, follow your intuition.

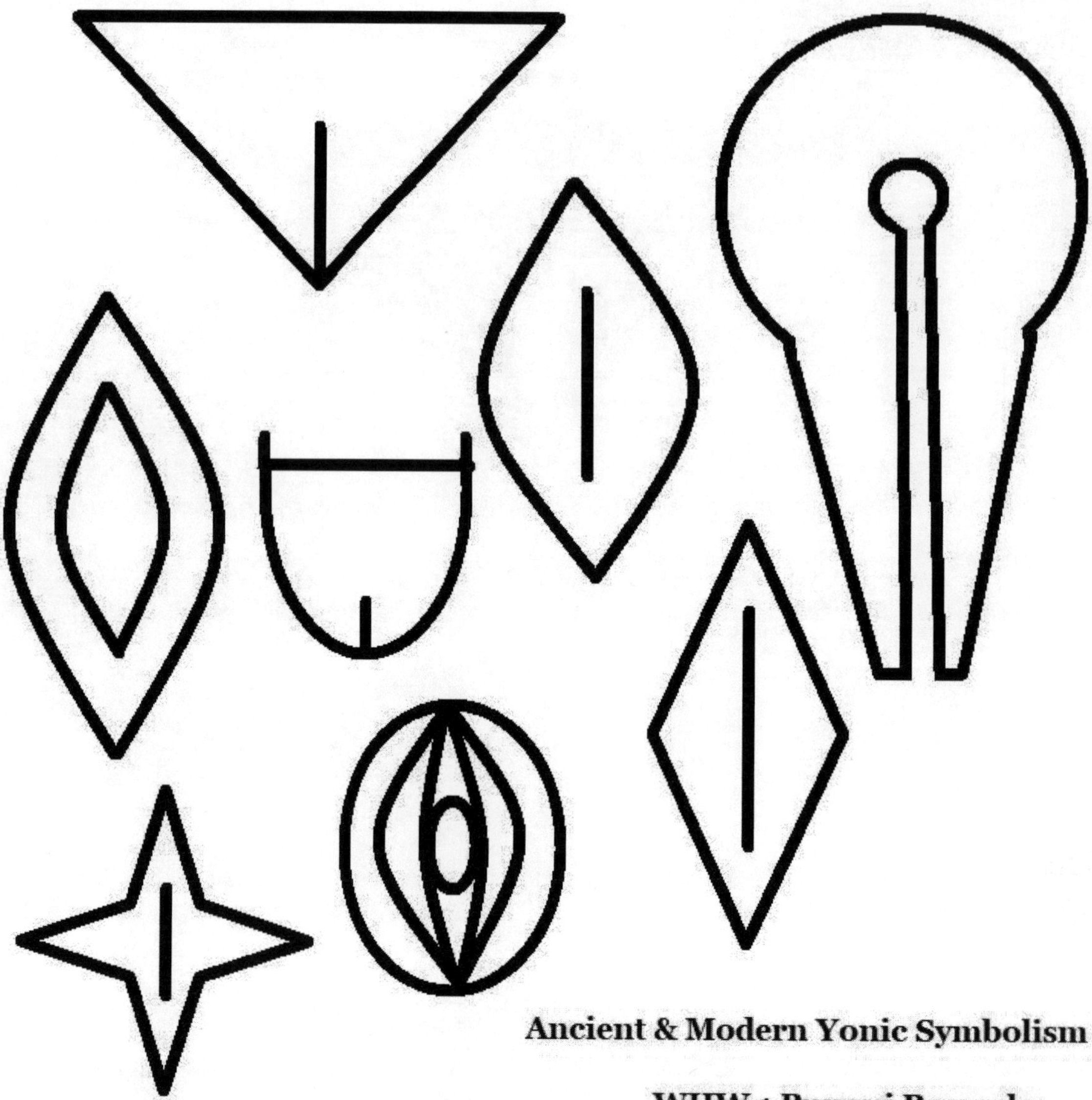

Ancient & Modern Yonic Symbolism

WHW 1 Punani Proverbs

Jot down any Punani candles you use and the dates used below:

Goddess Baths

No matter who you go to or what element you work with best, sacred, spiritual baths will probably always be suggested to you. This type of healing is powerful tool for spiritual and physical cleansing, coming back into your center of peace and positivity, washing away negative thoughts, gaining new ideas, thinking something over, clearing your mind, and talking to your Ancestors.

More commonly called a "spiritual" or "sacred" bath, this is a way of spending time with and on yourself. My suggestion is to bath between the hours of 4-6am for maximum clarity and openness to the spirit. Much of the healing comes from the very act of taking the time in your day to relax in the tub.

In a bath, water welcomes your entire body in. Water does not discriminate against any body type or body part. It touches and heals all equally, and reminds us to do the same when cherishing ourselves and our own bodies.

Showering is also healing and helpful, and these can also be made into sacred and healing experiences. My advice for a sacred Goddess Shower would be to utilize fresh herbs for maximum effect, as well as essential oils. Be sure the oils do not get on the floor, which can cause a slipping hazard. Use Goddess showers as time to meditate and pray, to allow water and scents to wash over you. Just as with a Goddess Bath, feel free to decorate your space with candles, incense, and other uplifting items.

For each of these baths, use what ingredients you have and of course use substitutions based on need, location, and personal tradition. The simple recipe to always follow is: name your purpose for taking this bath, then add botanicals and blessings. When you talk to and involve your Ancestors/Spirit Guides and add plants for ashe and spirit, you allow the bath to be truly special, unique, and powerful.

Do not forget to leave time to rest afterwards, as most Goddess Baths will leave you drained and exhausted.

Flora Bath - *Useful for directing plant energy. Also a way to connect with the land/city you are in.*

- Go outside and ask a few flowers and leaves to join you in your bath on your sacred journey of healing and wellness from the detox. Only take the ones that you are sure are energetically saying "yes" they will help.
- Rip them up small and add these to your goddess bath with a few drops of essential oils, keeping the bath simple, symbolic, and fresh.
- Flora should be as colorful as you can make the bath appear. Decorate the room with any extras.
- When you are finished, go rest.

Juvenated Bath - *Give energy the night before a big day/event.*

- Gather leaves only (small amount of wood is fine). Spinach, mint, or wild leaves are all acceptable.
- Fill the tub with water
- Fill a large bowl with half cold water, half milk (preferably coconut)

- Lean back, and submerge your body fully under the water whenever you feel called to during the bath. Allow yourself to float freely and relaxed there for several seconds before rising again.
- Rise from the water and go rest.

Cleansed & Prepared Bath - *Conquer diet or habits.*

- Boil a large pot of detox tea and let it brew overnight (or at least 3 hours).
- Run a hot bath. You can choose to strain the tea or not before adding it.
- Add fresh mint or mint essential oil to the water.
- If you do not suffer from high blood pressure, you can also choose to add 1-3 lbs of Epsom Salts, or 1 lb of Dead Sea Salt to your bath.
- Soak and pray.
- Halfway through, you can pour cold water with cayenne pepper and the juice of one lemon over your head.
- Be sure to shower off the salt after you are finished.
- When you are finished, make time to rest.

Ancestors Cover Me Bath - *Done during times of spiritual need.*

- Get 2 pitchers or bowls.
- In the first bowl, crack three eggs and mix with honey and water just until you have a pourable mixture.
- In the second, put some cinnamon and your favorite scent (oudh, fragrance) and cover with cool water.
- Draw a steaming hot bath. Pray over it. Ask for protection. Speak of what ails you and who wishes to harm you.
- After soaking some time, pray for cleansing and wellness from the Ancestors
- When ready, pour the egg and honey on your head. Allow it to wash over you and refresh your spirit, as well as moisturize your body. Feel rejuvenated in your Ancestor's presence and strength.

- Sit down in the water again, and then lay down and allow your entire head to submit under water. Float calmly for a moment under the water and feel calmed in the warmth that envelops you.
- Rise and meditate for some time on what you are trying to let go of and change, and what needs to happen for this to occur.
- When ready, pour the scented water over your head, envisioning the old you being washed away and your new strengthened self standing there instead.
- When you are ready, leave this bath and go pray or rest.

Fairest of Them All Bath - *Glamour bath for beauty, loveliness, femininity, and vitality.*

- Make a hibiscus, rose, rosemary and dandelion bath (or any combo of 1-3 of these). Hibiscus and Rose are mainstays in Glamour rituals--if you bath in them spiritually they enhance femininity, beauty, and general attractiveness. Rosemary fixes up a feminine persons home, represents love, fidelity, honesty and wisdom--traits you need whether you have a partner or not! A old Hoodoo practice tells wives to put a Rosemary plant on top of the shelf or fridge to control their house. Dandelion deals with growth and radiance (amongst other things), here with your inner self.
- Create an inviting bath using your favorite ingredients. Lean towards ones that make you feel alive, vivacious, flirty, confident, and thriving. This will vary, depending on the person.
- Soak and envision the water pulling out your sorrows, insecurities, and toxins. All negativity, all ugly, simply draining away.
- Envision confidence, self esteem, and beauty replacing it.
- After this bath, rub the body down with oils before moving on to resting or other activities.

Stayin your center by consistently taking cleansing baths. Self care should become second nature, and these baths (or showers, if that is what you have) are the perfect stress reliever if nothing else. Knowing when to utilize tools such as a spiritual bath will help you navigate both spiritual and physical stress. Try choosing one day a month to give yourself a spiritual bath...also consider utilizing them with family, such as your children or spouse, and also close friends.

Plan your own cleansing Goddess Bath, or plan them for your family:

Smoke Cleansing

As we touched on in the Womb Sauna section, another powerful method of cleansing both yourself and the space around you spiritually is smoke cleansing. All over the world you can research indigenous cultures utilizing smoke to push away unwanted energies and invite other ones in.

Using a fire safe bowl, charcoal, and dried herbs, incense, and resins, you can create your own smoke cleansing rituals at home.

Smoke Cleansing Herbs:

- Cedar
- Sage
- Lavender

- Rose Petals
- Pine
- Tobacco
- Sweetgrass
- Lemongrass
- Cinnamon
- Copal
- Palo Santo

Please research the herbs you use, as some (such as palo santo and white sage) are being overharvested and are threatened by endangerment and extinction. These should only be used if you have a bloodline connection or specific reason for using. Otherwise, there are a lot of other alternatives.

Notes:

Home Cleansing

"Know that all the good housekeeping you are performing is actually prayer in motion." • Queen Afua, *Sacred Woman*

Cleaning your home is important not only for physical wellness, but more importantly spiritual. As many of our Ancestors have quoted in various forms since ancient times, "Cleanliness is next to godliness".

This idiom means a lot more than many people think...For most it was the admonishment that grandmother gave to wash hands before supper.

To begin with, being clean is symbolic--it is symbolic of your spiritual devotion, purity, as well as goodness. When you wash with soap this cleanses the dirt and grime...when you wash with Florida Water, Blessing water, or similar equivalent, you cleanse yourself of energies that have accumulated around you. There are Gods and Goddesses who won't even respond to you if you have not taken the respectful gesture of washing yourself of grime and wayward energies before approaching them.

Further than that, we can remember that a clear space leads to a clear head. This is why the art of Feng Shui (or the use of the energy forces around us to harmonize individuals with their surrounding environment) is considered in such high regard by spiritual people. Some even go so far as to be minimalist, but I am sure most rootworkers, witches, and other spiritual workers find they end up collecting a lot of things that help them with their work.

When you want your home to feel more inviting and with better energy, try to get more natural light and air inside. When the air is stale and the lights are dim, it gives an impression of being clustered and held up, causing those inside to want to take a break elsewhere, if only to stretch.

Below I have included several ways you can cleanse your home spiritually as well as keep up with and build a good relationship with it.

Smoke Cleansing Plants:

- Tobacco
- Sage
- Cedar
- Sweetgrass
- Copal
- Pine
- Rosemary
- Cinnamon
- Peppermint
- Birch
- Rose

- Eucalyptus
- Lavender

Burn the herbs on a lit incense coal in a fireproof bowl or swinging incense lantern. You can also bundle the herbs together to create a thick stick to burn (around 1 inch diameter and 4+ inches in length).

Simple Cleansing Solution:

Take the peels of two oranges (or lemon, lime, clementine, etc) and put them in a jar so that they curl around the sides, colorful side facing out. You can choose to let the peels dry prior to putting them in vinegar to prevent molding.

Fill the jar with white vinegar and soak for 2+ weeks in a cabinet or dark space.

When you are ready to use, remove the orange peels and use in a spray bottle diluted 50/50 with water. Use for cleaning the home as you would use vinegar normally, and know the vinegar smell has been largely covered and reduced.

To Use Spiritually: Mix 1 part Orange Vinegar, 1 part Florida Water (recipe later in this chapter), and 2 parts water in a bowl. Wipe your home down from ceiling to floor. If other cleansers are necessary to wipe it down, use those first. Offer prayer and play spiritually charged music. Keep at least one window open a crack to allow energy to leave and air to freshen the home.

Caution: Many common types of citrus contain a cleaning agent called "d-limonene". This cleanser is used in many common household cleaners, *however* many people are sensitive to it on their skin, so be aware and use gloves if necessary.

Notes:

Stovetop Air Cleanser

To cleanse the air, smell, and atmosphere of your home all you need are some herbs, water, a pot and a stove (or crockpot)!

Boil the herbs for 5-10 minutes--adding more water if the liquid gets low--and you will be able to stir positive memories and emotions in the minds of all who walk through your home. If using a crockpot, turn it on high until you smell it, then keep it on low the rest of the day, checking periodically to ensure the water isn't getting too low. The effects can last for hours or even days depending on how strong your recipe is.

Freshen your home when you need to lighten the mood or energy, when you are cleaning the home, when you need inspiration, before rituals, or during celebrations/events.

Here are some basic recipes to inspire you throughout the year (feel free to substitute fresh herbs for essential oils and vice-versa):

<u>Spring:</u>

- 2 Lemons, sliced
- 2 sprigs of Rosemary
- 3+ cups of water
- 3 drops of peppermint extract

Summer:

- A splash of vanilla extract
- 2 sprigs of Thyme
- 4 Limes, sliced
- 2 sprigs of Mint
- 3+ cups of water

Autumn:

- 2 Apples, sliced
- 2 Cinnamon sticks
- Tablespoon Anise
- Tablespoon Nutmeg
- Splash of Vanilla Extract
- 3+ cups of water

Winter:

- 2 Oranges, sliced
- 1 cup Cranberries
- 3 Cinnamon sticks
- 12 whole cloves
- 3+ cups of water

When finished, pour the remaining product into a glass jar with a lid and put it into the fridge after each use. You can reuse around a week, replacing the fruit occasionally as it gets too brown.

Brainstorm your own recipes and take note of how they went:

Cinnamon Broom

> **"Take the finest spices: twelve pounds of liquid myrrh, half that amount (that is, six pounds) of sweet smelling cinnamon, six pounds of sweet smelling cane, and twelve pounds of cassia. Weigh all of these by the Holy Place measure. Also take four quarts of Olive oil, and mix all of these things like a perfume to make a holy olive oil. This special oil must be put on people and things to make them ready for service to God." Exodus 30:22-25**

Hung or leaned by the door, cinnamon brooms have long been used in Hoodoo and Folk Magic traditions…They are said to sweep away obstacles and negative energy from the home (or workplace) while drawing in luck and prosperity. The uplifting and joyous smell of cinnamon in the home gives a soulful, warm feeling to all who enter.

The use of brooms spiritually are found in Africa, where straw brooms are kept on altars, and this tradition carried throughout the Diaspora. Sweeping motions are often seen in ceremonial African and Diasporic dancing. The symbolism behind sweeping away the old/unfulfilling is even found in the

African American tradition of jumping the broom as well--the official wedding ceremony of enslaved black people who were not legally allowed to marry. Today a handmade or decorated broom is a powerful symbolic gift for a new couple or home.

Traditionally a handmade besom is made of pine and various cleansing herbs (such as sage or lavender) and after drying is then anointed with an special, thick, aromatic oil. The oil described at the beginning of this section in Exodus 30 gives you better idea of the concept of using a special blend of oils and herbs to create a rich and luxurious anointing liquid.

Whether in Exodus or conversation, people have long since been looking for ways to protect them self, their family, and their home. Protecting the home is exactly what anointing and utilizing a cinnamon broom is all about! Let the ancient recipe from the Bible inspire you in creating your own precious blend for a scented broom.

Ingredients:

- Broom (handmade or purchased)
    - Handmade: Gather twigs, grass, lavender, and other fibers, as well as a long stick. Soak the bristles first to soften them a little bit (different fibers will take different times). Blot dry them with a towel.
      Arrange as many fibers as you prefer around one end of the stick, not going passed the end and tie tightly in place with twine. Finally, fold the fibers into a downward position so they are now poking off of the end of the stick, arrange them nicely, and tie tightly again. Trim the ends to make it look uniform, if that is your preference.
- Cinnamon sticks and deep pot. Can add essential oils.
- *OR* Essential oils (cinnamon &/or 1-2 more such as hyssop, frankincense, myrrh, mint, or lotus)
    - You can also add a Condition Oil (an oil, made and blessed by a trusted spiritualist, that will aid a condition you are experiencing

or trying to experience--such as protection or prosperity). Allow your broom to work with you on multiple levels of home health!
    - If using more than 1, you will need a bowl to mix these in
- Charms, ribbons, herbs, bead strings, yarn and other items to personalize your broom. Add symbols and colors with meaning to you, as well as properties that work with your need. Pray over and consecrate each item...take the creation of this as the sacred spiritual tool that it is.
- Disposable gloves (cinnamon essential oil burns, as do many other essential oils)
- Plastic garbage bag
- A clean and peaceful workspace.

Remember that the meaning behind your choice of herbs, spices, and decoration should not only be based on other peoples interpretations but your personal experiences and preferences.

Take time to make your own special oil recipe for making a cinnamon broom that is unique to your home, and can be passed down through the bloodline! Write down the ingredients in the recipe in your journal for quick reference next time.

<u>Instructions</u>:

- If you *hand made* your broom, add the herbs while you are making it to the fibers on the bottom. You *must* allow the herbs to dry completely before adding the oils. Allowing the herbs and the broom to dry together, allows the ashe (energy) and properties of the plants to seep into the broom.
  If you *bought* your broom, attach herbs to the broom and stick them throughout the bristles, and allow them to dry while attached that way.
- When the broom is dry, go somewhere sacred where you can concentrate. Set up a space with whatever helps you get in the zone--smoke cleanse, light candles, make a small altar, turn on music.

- Call on your Ancestors to come into the space and join you, adding their spirit to your work. Invite Ancestors that knew how to keep a home, that were fierce protectors of their space and who was in it.
- Boil a large pot of water with 1-3+ cinnamon sticks. Remove when deep and smelling delicious and soak your broom for 4-8 hrs.
- Dry thoroughly in sunlight and/or fresh breeze

OR

- Take a small bowl and make a mixture of the oils you have chosen. Do not choose more than 2 if you are not familiar with mixing scents. Name your reason for adding each scent and drop of oil, and what you hope to gain from using your broom.
- Put on your gloves and using the oil, dress your broom. From the handle to each bristle, run your fingers over every surface. Be generous and abundant, just as you hope the blessings to be generous and abundant on their return.
    - As you work, pray, hum, and sing. Keep your mind and energy on your home and family, the joy they bring you, the wellness you pray upon them.
- When you are finished dressing the broom, carefully place it into a large plastic bag (2 if necessary), wrap it gently, and leave to soak for 2+ weeks

- When you remove the broom/it is dry, you can decorate it with your symbolic decor.
- Tie 9 ribbons around the handle of the broom, so they fall around the fibers of the broom head.
- Anoint the broom in oil/boil it 1-2x a year. To refresh it in between these times, simply boil water and hold it over the steam to reactivate the essential oils and dried herbal scents.

Start in the back of the home or room and sweep to the front, envisioning the old energy leaving and the blessings being swept in. If you have enemies or a bad house guest, sweep when they leave. When you need your neighbors to be sweeter, sweep blessings in their direction so their life becomes so good they don't bother with you anymore. Leave the broom at the door or on the porch.

Notes:

Florida Water

Good old “flowda wata” is a must-have around your home, especially as you transition into and begin to live a spiritual life daily. “Florida” comes from the Spanish word “florido” meaning “full of flowers”. You might’ve seen this product being sold in most botanicas and spiritual shops, both homemade and commercially made. It is wise to keep a bottle or two in your home for emergency purposes, especially one readily made by a trusted spiritualist, but this is an item you can make at home, and when it is homemade becomes that much more infused with your own spiritual power.

If you have time, make a few jars for your own home! Don't be afraid to add personal touches...I will add a few of my favorite suggestions below. As always, strive for fresh ingredients, but do not stress yourself if all you can get is dry. Use what you have. Many have 7+ ingredients, but keep it simple if that is what you prefer. Do what works for your personal ritual needs. Consider making different batches depending on the spiritual need.

Example Florida Water Recipe:

- Several cups of Vodka (or other 80 proof, clear liquor)
- 3 Cinnamon Sticks
- 20 Cloves
- Petals from a rose
- Sprigs of Jasmine
- Sprigs of Basil
- Sprigs of Lemongrass
- Heads of Lavender
- 2 Star Anise
- Some Orange, Lemon, or Grapefruit Peels
- A couple of Bay Leaves
- Patience and time.

Suggested Additions:

- Essential Oil, such as Ylang Ylang, Eucalyptus, Myrrh, or Sandalwood. Feel free to use your favorite scents.
- Local wildflowers and leaves gathered from around your town or city.
- Add a crystal to the jar during infusion stages, such as amethyst, rose or clear quartz, or obsidian. Research other crystals that might work for

your needs. Make sure that these crystals are not water soluble unless that is something you specifically are interested in.

Instructions:

- Begin by smoke cleansing your area, self, and tools
- Place the ingredients in the jar. Massage the herbs before placing inside the jar. Offer a prayer to the Ancestors as you do so. Speak freely from the heart, or say a chant or mantra (look below for suggestions).
- Pour the vodka onto the ingredients slowly and steadily. You can choose to just cover the herbs, or to completely immerse them in double the amount of liquor. Seal the jar as tight as you can with the lid.
- Hold the jar with one hand on the lid and the other on the bottom. Swirl the jar meditatively, infusing the healing energy of your Ancestors within it.
- Choose where you would like your Florida Water to infuse and charge. Preferably, you should dig a hole in some Earth and bury it (consider using a hidden place in a local wildlife park, if you are lucky enough to be near one!). You can also keep it in your closet or other dark space if your living situation simply doesn't allow it. You can choose to charge it under only the moonlight, or only the sunlight. You can choose to swirl your mixture according to the solar cycle, that is at noon and midnight. Whatever your choice, be purposeful and follow your intuition and do not be satisfied until months of work have been placed into your preparation for desired effect.
- Of course, write down your actions in your Book of Power.
- If pressed for time:
    - Heat the vodka *lightly* on the stove, then add the herbs. Cook for 30-45 min. Allow to cool and add to the jar to sit as long as possible.
- When finished, keep in the fridge.

- Mix with equal parts Rain or Spring water for use on body.

Florida Water is commonly known to remove negative energy, preparing people and items for blessings, encouraging people towards expression and emotion.

Using Florida Water:

- Wip down items on your altar, or other Sacred Space. Wipe down a room or new home if necessary.
- Wash the floors of your home to usher in prosperity and wellness. You can do this on Monday to honor your Ancestors, a tradition adopted by many who practice Hoodoo from the Vodou religion.
- Use a cup in the mop bucket or when washing the laundry.
- For a quick, basic, and simple spiritual cleanse, splash some Florida Water on your face and neck.
- Add several drops to a bowl of water to create a simple and effective blessing water for a ceremony, such as a sacred meeting or ritual.
- Make a refreshing, cleansing spray. Mix a few tablespoons into a spray bottle with water and additional essential oils of your choice. Spray on yourself, family, and friends in need. Spray down your rooms and chairs after an unpleasant guest leaves the house.
- Add a dash to your sacred Goddess Bath.
- Bath a cowrie shell in a bath of florida water. Sew/Add it to your clothes or wallet.
- Bless your sacred gathering by creating a spiritual circle made with libations of Florida Water (either pure or diluted with spring/rain/sea water)
- Use to pour libations or place as offering water at an altar.

- After moving into a new home, bless it and get to know it. In a bowl, mix preferred herbs (a common one is basil) and ice, anoint your doors, windows, and wash the floors to bring prosperity, safety, and love.

Notes:

Laundry Room

People *hate* the laundry room, and doing laundry (generally speaking). Some of us like to wash the clothes, but most try to avoid their laundry at all costs, detesting the process. I wondered even as a child why that was. All chores, after all, are annoying. Why is this one that we hear of the most?

Over the years I payed attention to laundry-related subjects, taking note when an elder advised me to keep my laundry area beautiful, so as to be inspired to use it and spend time there.

Later I learned something I think should have been obvious to me: *our clothes are what we wear in the outside world.* Meaning, just as much as anything, our clothes are picking up energy from whoever was around us at the time...and not just us! Whoever else lives with us and shares our laundry (spouse, children, parents, siblings, etc.) also mixes their energy with ours. When it sits in the laundry basket and then gets washed together, energy swirls together and can create a very depressing environment to be in.

Adding Florida Water (or your own special cleansing/herbal powder mix) to the laundry is an excellent way to cleanse the clothes spiritually while they are physically cleansing in the washer. Our Ancestors also used something called "bluing squares" which also acted as bleach and you can still purchase today, but be sure to dissolve completely in water or else you will stain your white clothes! These blue squares were also used as ink, dye, as well as in different traditional conjuring methods, however many factories are discontinuing their production due to lack of demand.

Working with a professional practitioner to create a sigil and protection shield for your laundry basket is also an alternative to look into to protect your space. Consider to yourself--are you (and your family, friends, visitors etc) inviting spirits and energies into your home through their clothing that you are not actively taking care of?

Notes:

Bless Your Home

Upon moving in or out of a home, do a small ceremony.

Initially, thank the home for taking you in. Thank it for covering your family, protecting you, and being support you could lean on. Bring a small gift. Place salt in the corners and clean it out physically and spiritually. Celebrate your entrance in the way that suits you best.

Take care of the home as a way of showing appreciation and reverence. Speak to the home when you need to. Show it you care. Give it a nickname!

When you are leaving, thank the home for having been there, good times and bad. Clean your DNA of the place. Sprinkle water in all corners after you are done. Leave something small offering, such as flowers. If the situation was tumultuous, you might be able to ask the home for help with the situation upon leaving (such as getting full deposit back, revenge on homeowner, etc).

Plan moving in/out rituals to honor the roof over your head:

Blessing Infused Oil

If we close our eyes right now, all Black folks have the memory ingrained in the back of their mind...storing tinctures and infusions in aging old liquor bottles...herbs floating serenely inside….

You have the same opportunities before you. Keep those old liquor bottles that you like and put them to the side, filling with your preferred infusing oil, creating blessing oils and waters, as well as tinctures and other mixtures for use when you reach that level in your knowledge. Try your best to use live/fresh herbs for these tinctures and infusions as these are the plants with Ashe/energy in them that will not have been handled by countless people before reaching you.

Always be cautious, especially if picking wild plants. Most blessing oils and waters are anointed on the face and body, so be sure to double check all gathered leaves and plants for safety reasons. There are apps that you can download to upload a picture of your plant and confirm its name and safety.

<u>Traditional infusions are simple and made with four ingredients:</u>

- A Glass Jar
- Extra Virgin Olive Oil, cold pressed (or other carrier, body moisturizing oil)
- Fresh and/or Dry Herbs of your choosing
- Time

Choose your herbs wisely! Do personal research, talk to an herbalist you trust (pay them for their time), and decide which herbs will work best for your family and situation. Cinnamon is known to bring prosperity. Chamomile, Lavender and California Poppy, for example, are all herbs that help with relaxation, rest, and sleep *and* are child safe. Hyssop is cleansing. Each of these could make a blessing oil for a different situation, and as a healer (of your family or professional) these are wonderful to keep on hand to use, send small vials with your children for their own personal use, anoint home items, and more.

To Make an Oil Infusion:

- Invite the Ancestors. Pray. Focus on what it is that you would like the tincture to do. Put your emotional energy into it.
- Fill the jar ⅓ to ½ way full of herbs. The more herbs you use, the stronger the infusion will be. Allow the herbs to be loose in there how they fall--do not pack them down.
- Fill the jar with the oil the rest of the way.
- Lid the jar and bury in the earth (or leave in a cool, dark place).
- Shake periodically every 2-4 weeks if buried *or* daily for 6-10+ weeks.
- Pray with it periodically. Allow to bath under the New or Full moon cycle of an entire year. Look through the jar at the sun or moon. Place on your altar. Inspire yourself and follow your intuition on how to work with your infusion.

- When you and it are ready, you can strain the herbs out through a metal strainer if you prefer to take them out.
- Store in a liquor bottle or other dark/colored glass.

Use for anointing people, dressing candles and other items,

Notes:

Womb/Healing Teas

Teas have long since been a way for people to self medicate in the home. You can utilize teas to help promote circulation, give vitamins, ease symptoms from menstrual cycle, birth, or lactation, connect you with a particular ancestor, and simply to warm you up.

Be careful of using detoxing herbs while breastfeeding or pregnant, as the detoxed material can easily get transferred to the child. *Always check any herbs going inside your body, including those on this list, to know the best times to properly use them by yourself.* Check and triple check-- you and I are not herbalists, and nothing but the most basic herbs should be used in your teas unless you are more well studied, no matter how simple or safe the herb/process might seem.

Pregnancy, Breastfeeding, and Womb Safe Herbs:

- Red Raspberry Leaf
- Cinnamon
- Hibiscus
- Lemon Balm
- Nettles
- Lady's Mantle
- Peppermint
- Dandelion

Notes:

As you experiment with each, alone and together, write your own recipes:

Womb Massage

When your womb aches or has pains, you notice and take action, right? Pills, cannabis, hot water bottles, sleep. The common remedies for womb pain are endless, yet none of them seem to involve actually reaching down and touching it yourself.

“Laying hands” as it is commonly called today is an ancient practice that dates back to before Christianity, when pagan customs ruled the earth. The placing of hands on someone and calling for spiritual and divine aid or healing is a powerful act, and this healing has been witnessed for many century and generations. Another popular method of laying hands today is called “reiki”, which again people train to do for others in their community. Why then do people avoid laying hands on themselves?

Release any fears or inhibitions. You do not need to be any more of a professional to massage your womb than you need to be pro to massage your own sore neck. Simply grab your favorite oil, such as olive, and find a comfortable and serene place to lay on your back with your womb exposed.

The womb is around 4 fingers down from your belly button. With your hands covered lightly in a blessed (or prayed over) oil, smoothly and lightly run your fingers and palms over your womb. Try to feel it under your hands, but if you cannot, trust it is there.

Don't be afraid to be firm! This isn't a deep tissue massage, but that doesn't mean you should barely touch the skin. Find a nice medium, find what *you* enjoy. Focus on your pelvis and joints, all the way up even to your belly button. Try to pull the belly and skin up as you massage, not down. Use as much oil as needed to truly moisturize and pamper your cracks, curves, rolls.

As you spend this time, hum a song of healing to your womb. Hum deeply, from within your chest and soul. Feel the vibrations of your melody reverberate through each cell of your body as you gently massage your creative chamber. Maybe this melody you hum is the familiar heart song you naturally start to sing when you get to being musical. Maybe it is one someone you once knew used to sing. Maybe it is a song you only learned recently, but speaks out to your bloodline. Whatever you hum, let it be natural. No one is here to judge your communication with your womb. You are here to take this journey together, one step at a time, twin deer out for their first walk…

As you hum, consider. Consider how far you've come, and how much you have grown. Consider what you'd like for the future. Consider what needs to be released to get there. Consider what you are willing to release...what you have released in the past. Was it worth it? Can you do it again?

Feel your womb beneath your fingers. Feel the strength and pulsing light. This energy within you is vital and raw. It is power. There are infinite possibilities, each more intriguing than the last. Which will you be choosing?

Remind yourself that spiritual growth *is* very hard work….how much effort are you willing to put in?

As you finish your womb massage, begin to imagine that your fingertips are filled with a small light….the color is whichever you feel in that moment gives you the most power and vitality.

With your eyes closed, watch it begin seeping down and rooting out within your womb, expanding slowly outward. Eventually the light encases your womb and begins to spill its roots out into your body, slowly working its way down to your toes and up to your brain. Down your arms the light goes until finally it touches your fingers through your hands, creating a swirling flow of powerful healing energy connecting your womb, heart, and mind. You are one, your womb and you. Your energy and you. Your bloodline and you.

When you finish giving yourself a natural and intuitively led massage, rest and relax for some time afterwards. Be in no rush to rise again. Appreciate any emotions you might be feeling during this encounter.

As you continue to practice womb massage, you will find what works best for you. If you feel you need a more professional hand assisting your womb, locate a traditional womb massager in your area...many advertise their services through the web. It is always wise to determine which parts of your trauma and pain are beyond your personal abilities for healing, and then delegate accordingly.

Reflect:

Pendulum

Pendulum Reading

A tool that served as my first form of "divination" and a huge help for my growth in self knowledge and healing was learning to read a pendulum.

A pendulum is a weight suspended from a string or chain so that it can swing freely. It can be used to read energy and answer a question with your own intuition. A pendulum is only a tool to aid with ease and clarity of the answers--it is useful especially for when you can't quiet your mind, make a decision, need to follow your heart, or are trying to be clear and concise. It is great for people who need visuals as well.

Either purchase a pendulum or make one by putting something heavy on the end of a string, or simply use a necklace with a weighted charm on the end. The string or chain should be around 6" long, and does *not* need to be longer. Hold the pendulum comfortably in your fingers.

Establish the answer "yes" by asking the pendulum to rotate in a clockwise direction. Do *not* move your hand; use only the energy from your thoughts.

Ask it to stop, or show you "void" and wait for it to still. Establish "no" by having it rotate in a circle counterclockwise, opposite of yes. Have the pendulum stop. Last, establish "neutral" by having the pendulum sway back and forth from you, or to and away.

The pendulum can be a powerful tool of self divination and discernment. It can challenge your perceptions of your health and wellness, and serve as a neutral guide to your own inner intuition. Try not to ask the pendulum in a state of anguish and high emotion, but rather in a wiser place of seeking the honest truth for the overall betterment of self. It is not a tool for divining the future, but rather for divining yourself.

<u>Example Questions for Your Pendulum:</u>

Am I afraid of my feelings?

Will I know myself better after doing this exercise?

What age am I emotionally halted at? (Count rotations)

Am I angry (sad, disappointed) in __________?

Does she blame me for what happened?

Is this a healthy food for my body/womb at this time? (hold pendulum over food)

Will doing __________ benefit my womb?

Should I do this cleansing bath/ritual tonight?

Is my stress over this causing my headaches?

Hold the pendulum over your womb, heart, and mind to read a positive, negative, void, or neutral reading. Note how fast or slow the pendulum moves, or how many times it spins.

Womb Energy Reading

- Take out your womb journal (or lut a notebook into your Book of Power) to write down the day, date, and time.
- Use your pendulum to scan your entire body from head to toe, both physically and spiritually. Write down the results (Positive, Negative, Adverse, or Void). Be sure to include if the pendulum moved energetically or sluggishly).
- Using tarot or other divination card deck, pull 4 cards. Ask:
  - Where is my womb physically right now?
  - Where is my womb emotionally right now?
  - Where is my womb spiritually right now?
  - What is the biggest thing I need to work on for my own healing?
- (Feel free to pull up to 5 more cards of a full sized deck to ask questions that are specific to your needs for that reading).
- Using a final divination method, ask for a general womb reading with it.
  - Use bone & curio reading, tea leaf reading, bibliomancy, charm divination, runes, casting lots etc.
- Record your results.

Reflect:

Womb Massage

When your womb aches or has pains, you notice and take action, right? Pills, cannabis, hot water bottles, sleep. The common remedies for womb pain are endless, yet none of them seem to involve actually reaching down and touching it yourself. Many get so caught up in buying tools and wanting something more, when really no purchase is necessary to work your energy and power.

"Laying hands" as it is commonly called today is an ancient practice that dates back to before Christianity, when pagan customs ruled the earth. The placing of hands on someone and calling for spiritual and divine aid or healing is a powerful act, and this healing has been witnessed for many centuries and generations. Another popular method of laying hands today is called "reiki", which again people train to do for others in their community. Why then do people avoid laying hands on themselves?

Release any fears or inhibitions. You do not need to be any more of a professional to massage your womb than you need to be pro to massage your own sore neck. Simply grab your favorite oil, such as olive and find a comfortable and serene place to lay on your back with your womb exposed.

The womb is around 4 fingers down from your belly button. With your hands covered lightly in a blessed (or prayed over) oil, smoothly and lightly run your fingers and palms over your womb. Try to feel it under your hands, but if you cannot, trust it is there.

Don't be afraid to be firm! This isn’t a deep tissue massage, but that doesn't mean you should barely touch the skin. Find a nice medium, find what you enjoy. Focus on your pelvis and joints, all the way up even to your belly button. Try to pull the belly and skin up as you massage, not down. Use as much oil as needed to truly moisturize and pamper your cracks, curves, rolls.

As you spend this time, hum a song of healing to your womb. Hum deeply, from within your chest and soul. Feel the vibrations of your melody reverberate through each cell of your body as you gently massage your creative chamber. Maybe this melody you hum is the familiar heart song you naturally start to sing when you get to being musical. Maybe it is one someone you once knew used to sing. Maybe it is a song you only learned recently, but speaks out to your bloodline. Whatever you hum, let it be natural. No one is here to judge your communication with your womb. You are here to take this journey together, one step at a time, twin deer out for their first walk…

As you hum, consider. Consider how far you've come, and how much you have grown. Consider what you'd like for the future. Consider what needs to be released to get there. Consider what you are willing to release...what you have released in the past. Was it worth it? Can you do it again?

Feel your womb beneath your fingers. Feel the strength and pulsing light. This energy within you is vital and raw. It is power. There are infinite possibilities, each more intriguing than the last. Which will you be choosing?

Remind yourself that spiritual growth is very hard work….how much effort are you willing to put in?

As you finish your womb massage, begin to imagine that your fingertips are filled with a small light….the color is whichever you feel in that moment gives you the most power and vitality.

With your eyes closed, watch it begin seeping down and rooting out within your womb, expanding slowly outward. Eventually the light encases your womb and begins to spill its roots out into your body, slowly working its way down to your toes and up to your brain. Down your arms the light goes until finally it touches your fingers through your hands, creating a swirling flow of powerful healing energy connecting your womb, heart, and mind. You are one, your womb and you. Your energy and you. Your bloodline and you.

When you finish giving yourself a natural and intuitively led massage, rest and relax for some time afterwards. Be in no rush to rise again. Appreciate any emotions you might be feeling during this encounter.

As you continue to practice womb massage, you will find what works best for you. If you feel you need a more professional hand assisting your womb, locate a traditional womb massager in your area...many advertise their services through the web. It is always wise to determine which parts of your trauma, and pain are beyond your personal abilities for healing, and then delegate accordingly.

Reflect:

Pendulum

Pendulum Reading

A tool that served as my first form of "divination" and a huge help for my growth in self knowledge and healing was learning to read a pendulum.

A pendulum is a weight suspended from a string or chain so that it can swing freely. It can be used to read energy and answer a question with your own intuition. A pendulum is only a tool to aid with ease and clarity of the answers--it is useful especially for when you can't quiet your mind, make a decision, need to follow your heart, or are trying to be clear and concise. It is great for people who need visuals as well.

Either purchase a pendulum or make one by putting something heavy on the end of a string, or simply use a necklace with a weighted charm on the end. The string or chain should be around 6" long, and does not need to be longer. Hold the pendulum comfortably in your fingers.

Establish the answer "yes" by asking the pendulum to rotate in a clockwise direction. Do not move your hand; use only the energy from your thoughts. Ask it to stop, or show you "void" and wait for it to still. Establish "no" by having it rotate in a circle counterclockwise, opposite of yes. Have the pendulum stop. Last, establish "neutral" by having the pendulum sway back and forth from you, or to and away.

The pendulum can be a powerful tool of self divination and discernment. It can challenge your perceptions of your health and wellness, and serve as a neutral guide to your own inner intuition. Try not to ask the pendulum in a state of anguish and high emotion, but rather in a wiser place of seeking the honest truth for the overall betterment of self. It is not a tool for divining the future, but rather for divining yourself.

Example Questions for Your Pendulum:

Am I afraid of my feelings?

Will I know myself better after doing this exercise?

What age am I emotionally halted at? (Count rotations)

Am I angry (sad, disappointed) in __________?

Does she blame me for what happened?

Is this a healthy food for my body/womb at this time? (hold pendulum over food)

Will doing __________ benefit my womb?

Should I do this cleansing bath/ritual tonight?

Is my stress over this causing my headaches?

Hold the pendulum over your womb, heart, and mind to read a positive, negative, void, or neutral reading. Note how fast or slow the pendulum moves, or how many times it spins.

Womb Energy Reading

Take out your womb journal (or lut a notebook into your Book of Power) to write down the day, date, and time.

Use your pendulum to scan your entire body from head to toe, both physically and spiritually. Write down the results (Positive, Negative, Adverse, or Void). Be sure to include if the pendulum moved energetically or sluggishly).

Using tarot or other divination card deck, pull 4 cards. Ask:

Where is my womb physically right now?

Where is my womb emotionally right now?

Where is my womb spiritually right now?

What is the biggest thing I need to work on for my own healing?

(Feel free to pull up to 5 more cards of a full sized deck to ask questions that are specific to your needs for that reading).

Using a final divination method, ask for a general womb reading with it.

Use bone & curio reading, tea leaf reading, bibliomancy, charm divination, runes, casting lots etc.

Record your results.

Reflect:

Crystal Charging Ritual

There are so many ways to charge a crystal! Bathing in the sun and moonlight, prayer, dipping into blessed or salt water, placing in the soil, just to name a few. This is just one way that I personally enjoy that I saw once done by a Gullah Geechee Witchdoctor. It's simple, but powerful and connective, and requires your attention, as well as your energy and other parts of your altar, which is a lot of why I like it.

- Place a tealight in the center of your palm on your right hand.
- Light it.
- Surround it by the crystals you would like to charge.
- Pray and sing over it, watching the flame
- Feel the heaviness in your palm and note any differences. Become familiar with these feelings over time.
- Allow the tea light burn as long as you can.
- Place the crystals on your altar

Notes:

Healing Salts

Salt is an ultimate purifier. When you combine this simple spice with other healing herbs, the result is a powerful infusion and all-purpose healer. The following recipe can be used inside your food, in your goddess baths, in your laundry (and hamper), in the corners of your home, when working roots, and more.

Tools:

- Sea Salt, Himalayan Pink Salt, or Celtic Salt (or other specialty salt)
- Fresh or Dried Herbs (fresh tends to be tastier)
    - Ex: Oregano, Citrus Peel, Garlic, Rosemary, Basil, Thyme, Rose Petal, Dandelion, Lavender, Sage, Cilantro, Dill, Parsley
- Mortar and Pestle
    - Food Processor can be used
- Glass jar

Directions:

- Decide how salty or herbal you want your mixture to be, and add salt and herbs intuitively.
- Grind together until mixed well, ground fine, and infused. (Salt will likely absorb the color of the plants). Focus on intent while grinding.
- Store in glass container.

Notes:

2 Item Altars:

In the spirit and honor of simplicity, minimalism, and a shortage of space and privacy, I thought I would cover the smaller altars. It's often easy to go big, large and wild. Spending lots of money and showering a situation with wealth and privilege is easy. Conveying a powerful message with just a few symbols is not.

Make small altars wherever you feel the urge...on window sills, in cars, outside. Spread your spirit.

Oil Lamp & Sacred Text

The text can be your grimoire, your current reading, guidance cards, a book written by the Ancestors, any reading you want to take more seriously.

Oil Lamps are a traditional lighting method that our Ancestors used for working roots. They also are a lot cheaper than candles in the long term, as well as safer. You can make them from clay for even more money saving, and even put your fresh/dried herbs, Condition oils, charms, petitions and more in the oil at the bottom!

Wood & Rocks

The perfect outdoor and large scale altar is the use of rocks and wood from the local area. Arrange them purposefully and leave a sacred place for others who pass by.

This could also be scaled down and brought inside to have a rearrangeable altar space.

2 Shells

Keep it simple! Use two shells (or another item) that hold purpose for you. Let them symbolically represent a word, phrase or mantra. Use the bumps and grooves like prayer beads. Then place the warm shells back in their place on the altar.

The Petals of 2 Flowers

A temporary, yet lovely altar is simply two flower petals arranged in a pleasing way. Leave these on a path while hiking, in a clearing, on a bench, on the sidewalk, or in a field of a local park.

2 Cups

Tie two cups together (handmade, or just two you cherish). Fill one with water and one with dry food. Or, fill one with special objects and the other with sacred tools. Or place crystals in one, and vignettes in the other. Use one for incense and the other for casting lots. The possibilities are endless!

Incense and a Statue

Find a statue that represents your Ancestors, Deity(s), or Spirit Guides. Honor and spend time around it regularly, lighting incense, herbs, resin, or candles as part of the ceremony.

Citrus & Cloves

My final suggestion includes 2 items found in most modern homes: whole cloves and oranges. When cloves are stuck into the orange and left to dry they create an amazing aroma together. Stick the cloves in to make specific shapes, symbols, and sigils, or simply cover the whole thing...create a bunch of these and keep them in a bowl. For enhanced aroma, make a small mixture of powdered cinnamon, cloves, nutmeg, allspice, anise, and orris root and roll the cloved orange in them.

Brainstorm your own 2 item altars:

Womb Crystals

Yoni Egg Crystal

Yoni eggs are a traditional method of connecting with your secret space that have become wildly popular in the last decade.

They have been around for centuries, beginning in ancient China with traditional jade eggs used by the royalty and concubines of the palace to tone, strengthen and please their sacred vaginal chambers….as well as, of course, provide the emperor with sweet snatch not found easily elsewhere. **Today dozens of different stones are used to make Yoni eggs, allowing for you**

to choose carefully the crystal properties to accompany your physical healing journey.

To use (following a small bonding period, see info on this later in this section), you simply take the crystal egg and place it at your vaginal lips, allowing it to slowly be inserted and enveloped by your vaginal canal. Through using your own fingers and/or vaginal muscles, you allow the egg to go as far back as you can in the vagina.

The walls of your vagina will naturally mold around the crystal, holding it up in place. The movement of the crystal, as well as the natural reflex of the vagina to hold it in, is a simple extension of vaginal exercise--or Punanilates as we call it earlier in this book. With the egg within, you can allow it to rest in your body and go about your normal daily life. Your vagina uses the muscles to hold the egg inside, building up strength as it becomes used to the exercise.

There is no fear of the egg becoming lost or stuck inside of you--the vaginal canal is not a long continuous open space. Rather, the vaginal walls typically touch each other when nothing is inside, opening to allow what is inserted. The cervix cannot take the egg inside, either, even on your period. It is recommended to remove the egg once your period begins, and not reinsert until the bleeding cycle is over.

Common Questions:

What happens if the crystal egg goes far in the back and will not come out? What if it stays there for days? What if I use my finger and it won't come out?	Relax. The egg will come out when it is ready...perhaps it recognizes you have a lot more work to do that it can help with energetically. Perhaps it is comfortable with you in your womb space. Perhaps your body is trying to connect with the crystal

	more closely. These are not reasons to be overly concerned. There is no harm in your yoni egg being within your womb for days or even weeks. If you absolutely must get it out right now, make sure you are in a calm state. Get into a good squatting position and try pushing it out with your vaginal muscles. If it doesn't seem like it is working, take a small break and then try this again. Use your fingers if you need to, but be gentle to the soft tissues inside.
What do I do if the crystal will not stay in, no matter how many times I try?	If the crystal will not stay inside your body, it could be that your muscles aren't ready to handles this. Try using a bigger stone, and working with it at smaller increments. Try using it while laying down to start. Your body could also be releasing the crystal because it has an energy you are not ready for, or really don't need. Use your intuition to guide you regarding your relationship with the crystals in your collection. Make the intimacy reciprocal.
Can I use a crystal vaginally if I am using an IUD?	No! Your crystal can (and probably will) knock your IUD out of place, especially if you have any type of insertive vaginal sex. The Mirena coil is especially prone to this.
What if I have a UTI, an STD, or	If you are experiencing infections,

other irritation or infection? Can I use a crystal?	open sores, or other irritation, *stop all use* until your illness clears up. Using a crystal during this time will not cure you physically and can cause spreading or exacerbate your discomfort.
If I find out I am pregnant, can I use a yoni egg?	Get clearance from your doctor, however for optimal safety, *only* use your crystal vaginally during pregnancy *if* you have *already been using for at least a year prior*. If your body has not been regularly accustomed to pelvic exercises and internal use of eggs, put it away until around 3-4 months postpartum.
Can I use a crystal egg inside of my vagina while on my period?	This is not recommended. Please allow your blood to flow out of your womb unobstructed during the few days of menstruation.

When choosing your yoni egg, whether it is your 1st or your 50th, always use your intuition. There are common stones most people use to start their journey, but I will not state them here because people's yoni egg journey's are all over the internet for you to see, and I think if you just make sure the crystal you choose is safe to use within your body, you will be just fine. Take your time, browse, and when you see the right one in your price range, you will know this is the crystal to use for your journey.

If you find yourself caught up in all of the options available and absolutely unable to make a decision, I would narrow down to your favorites, then Cast Lots--that is, write the names of each on a slip of paper, put them in a bowl, swirl around, and draw out one piece. Whichever crystal is written on the paper you choose, you would buy.

Egg Size Chart

Large	Larger eggs are for people who are beginning their yoni egg journey. The larger shape is not only easier to hold in, but also easier to notice when it is slipping out. Lastly, this egg is easier for a beginner to learn to push out of their vagina effectively--especially helpful for those who are afraid it is "stuck" or will get "lost" in there.
Medium	As you become more advanced in the technique of holding and releasing the egg will become easier...this is where the "medium" size comes in. Using a medium egg may be difficult if it is your first egg size, but it is possible.
Small	The smaller the egg, the more difficult it will be for a beginner or intermediate user to keep within their sacred space. Small yoni eggs allow you to place more than one inside of your vagina for combined crystal healing, as well as advanced toning.

Note:
- If your egg falls out of your yoni and into the toilet, DO NOT FLUSH the toilet because it will be gone forever! Use a glove and take it out, then clean it well.
- Yoni eggs should not be used with a diaphragm, tampon, menstrual cup, or on your period.

Cleansing your yoni egg should consist of placing it inside of a bowl or cup (preferably the same one every time...one just for cleansing crystals and altar items). Place with it some herbs and a few drops of essential oils, or let it sit alone, and pour hot (*not* boiling!) water over the egg while whispering a prayer, good intentions, or a positive mantra. Allow it to rest there and *completely cool down* before inserting it inside of your vagina.

As I mentioned above, some crystals should *not* be used inside of your punani! Keep this in mind, just because a crystal you see is shaped like an egg, or even if the seller insists it is one, some crystals are just plain unhealthy to insert in the body for various reasons. That does not mean they cannot be used, only that they should not be used internally.

Below you will find a chart of the most common toxic crystals sold in egg form, but please be sure to research the minerals that all of your eggs are comprised of before purchase to be sure, especially if you haven't seen many people with that egg before. It could be you stumbled on something wonderful and new, but it is more likely that there is a good reason, and you need to be safe.

Toxic Yoni Eggs

Crystal:	*Why It is Toxic For Internal Use:*
Fluorite	This one has the problem in the name...**fluoride**! Too much fluoride can lead to osteoporosis, irritation, and even death. This glassy egg tends to come in an

	array of beautiful colors from bright oranges and greens, to purples and grays. Very clear and vibrant colors. Sometimes also called “fluorspar” (“fluo” meaning “to flow” in Latin), this crystal is excellent for protective use against outside harms, especially negative energies that begin to rule relationships.
Hematite	This is a gorgeous egg that often looks like a dinosaur egg. This stone is very metallic, however, and *will* **rust** if placed in a moist environment such as your yoni. Sometimes these eggs are pure silver in color (making them tempting purchases for your spiritual journey) and others are mixtures of purple, pink green, or silver. Sleep with hematite under your pillow when especially stressed or worried to help alleviate these feelings.
Labradorite	This stone has **pyrite** and **sulfur**, both of which can lead to heart failure and make it hard for you to breath. This egg is another iridescent one with metallic tones and hints of blue and yellow as it reflects in the light. Get a labradorite pendulum or place one on your altar to increase intuitive abilities.

Lapis Lazuli	Lapis Lazuli also has **sulfur**, which gives it the unique color. A bright and welcoming royal blue, the Lapis Lazuli may also have traces golden flecks, which are the **pyrite** you see. Hold one of these stones in each palm when meditating or manifesting, and use a Blue Quartz instead.
Moonstone	I know, it's a beautiful and popular stone! Moonstone is actually a potassium-aluminum silicate, not a gemstone as the jewelry industry uses it. **Aluminum** is something the body needs 0% of, so your body can begin to accumulate it throughout the body, including in the brain. The Moonstone is usually an iridescent white, but can also be gray/silver. Wear a Moonstone necklace to bring a sense of balance, femininity, and wholeness to your everyday life, and choose a White Jade egg for the milky moon appearance instead.
Rhodochrosite	With its lovely light pink color it seems like this stone could be the perfect alternative to a Rose Quartz in your collection. The tiny black specks that decorate it, however, are **lead**, and most modern humans understand that lead poisoning can lead to pains,

	constipation, fatigue, hearing loss, and memory loss. Tuck one of these in your bag to give confidence before something big.
Selenite	Another glowing white egg that could be tempting to purchase is Selenite. Sadly, this stone **dissolves** in water, making it perfect for making blessing or ceremonial water...but not so much for the yoni. Try placing these in the 4 corners of your home, or on windowsills for protection instead.
Sodalite	Another lovely blue egg, Sodalite also contains **aluminum** and is considered a toxic crystal for internal use. Sodalite is a creative stone, perfect to use when you need to expand your mind for a project. More safe blue egg suggestions include Apatite and Blue Amethyst.
Tiger's Eye	The **asbestos** in Tiger's Eye also makes it one you should skip. Asbestos directly leads to cancers, something you are trying to avoid by healing your womb in the first place. Tiger's eye is a striped mixture of honey to deep browns, and is perfect to hold when making a big decision.

Other Yoni Crystals

Eggs are a popular shape for using internally, but they are not the only option.

As you begin to get better at holding smaller and smaller crystals in your yoni, you may be tempted to put several inside...or you could get a set of yoni spheres instead!

Yoni Spheres can be found sold one at a time or in pairs, and are usually used in sets of two. A higher level of expertise, these probably will not be held successfully inside unless you have at least already moved down to a medium, but preferably small yoni egg.

The toning and exercise are amplified with two spheres, and one of the best parts is that you can mix and match stones while using them.

The other common yoni crystal is the Yoni Wand or Lingam Wand. These are used for self pleasure as well as the toning effect. One thing generally uplifted about the Yoni Wand is that it is usually shaped at only 4-6 or so inches. This is because the need to have the largest/thickest penis within the yoni for orgasm is a relatively recent occurrence. Not all black people with penises have one that is 8+ inches, and not only that, but not all vaginas need a large one to orgasm! Using a yoni wand can open your eyes to what actually makes your vagina turned on and cum, as opposed to what is mainstream or expected.

Notes:

Bonding With My Yoni Eggs
Mini Journal

(When you get a new yoni egg, don't just stick it in your yoni...take the time to bond with it! Below are some suggestions. Fill in the blanks below to record your personal journey. Try to do at least 4 bonding exercises energetically with the crystal before insertion every time. This is how you can get your Ashe (energy) into it!)

Suggestions For Bonding:

- Sleep with the egg under your pillow
- Smoke cleanse it
- Put it on your womb, ancestor, or personal altar.
- Give it a personal name
- Take it in your sacred Goddess Bath
- Give it an herbal bath
- Put it in an indoor plant on the earth.
- Give a sun or moon bath.
- Do a ritual with it.
- Put it on or in front of your Self-Love Jar to charge and rest.

1)

Type of Crystal:	Date Acquired:

2)

Type of Crystal:	Date Acquired:

3)

Type of Crystal:	Date Acquired:

4)

Type of Crystal:	Date Acquired:

5)

Type of Crystal:	Date Acquired:

6)

Type of Crystal:	Date Acquired:

7)

Type of Crystal:	Date Acquired:

Releasing Your Yoni Eggs

Your connection with your egg can (and for the price they are, *should*) be deep, loving, and personal. Be creative and symbolic. Attach specific trauma to them. Purchase them for specific reasons. Spend years with them.

And yes. Someday, years from now--at the end of the road on one path….On the great beginning of your steps decisively to another….At a great aftermath of something, or at the ending stage of your grief--you might get the calling. The calling to release your Yoni Egg.

Bury your egg in the city that calls you.

Wake up and do not speak until the stone is buried. Wear all white, and choose one item to wear in your power color. Find a secluded spot and dig. Be it sand or soil, go far down enough that the stone will have time to heal. This act is not about the stone being found. Give the crystal back to whom it came. Let Mother Earth receive the trauma into the soil to cleanse on Her own terms. Let yourself be done with it. *Leave no trace.*

Go somewhere entirely different in the same city. You must still have natural earth beneath your feet, but you must not be within eye distance of where the stone is buried. This area too should be private.

Place 4 candles to represent the 4 directions. Pour libations to the Ancestors and pray, thanking them for their help in releasing this trauma, expressing gratitude for what is already here. Meditate, dance, play music, enjoy yourself. Remain until the candles burn out, or as long as you can. Leave no trace.

Notes:

Curses and Reciprocity

As the Punani giveth, so shall it taketh away! No, but really do you shy away from the destruction your womb can produce? You shouldn't. Things needed to be torn down, die, and come to an end in order for something else new, thriving, and more honorable to take its place.

Just like people get stuck on the idea of being happy, "full of light", and joyful all the time without acknowledging or respecting darkness as viable and even healthy, people also get caught in the cycle of wanting to endlessly create and have abundance without remembering that there something must be given with all of that taking. Balance is key, and the ability to not only end something, but to know *when* to end it is an intuitive skill that is only built through practice and honesty.

Earlier, we did a self-love jar, so it feels fitting that we also do a jar that works the opposite type of energy. In Hoodoo there is no Rule Of Three, "karma", etc. In fact, karma is an Asian concept referring to your actions affecting previous and future lives and has no bearing on most spiritualities outside of Asian ones. When people say "what goes around comes around" they actually are referring to the law of reciprocity.

Yes, if you curse people for fun, pick on folks, steal, or act fraudulently you *will* end up with enemies! And they in turn will try and fight back with all they have...these are natural consequences. But as for the average person, you are well within your rights to protect yourself, stand up for yourself, seek justice for yourself, and of course do the same for your family, friends, and community.

Be warned that curses and similar Work are higher level magic. If you have not done any other rootwork before, don't put any effort it the Ancestors, and are in most respects a beginner, there is a much larger chance that it can and will backfire on you. If the situation is serious, you have not had adequate preparation, and you are unsure, hire a spiritual worker to help or do the Work for you.

"First They're Sour, Then They're Frozen" Jar

Tools:

- 1 glass jar with lid
- 1 lemon
- 1 slip of paper
- 3-9 nails (can use paper clips, needles, staples, etc)
- Vinegar
- Freezer

Directions:

- Play appropriate music that gets you in the right frame of mind.
- Spend time dredging up the emotions that brought you here. Remember any stories, situations, or circumstances that require this intervention. Feel your emotions fully, decide what specifically you want to happen. Don't let go of your intent throughout the entire ritual.
- Write the name of the person, business, or organization you are targeting on the slip of paper. Use more than one lemon and/or several jars if necessary.
- Cut the lemon in half.
- Place the small paper inside the two halves completely and connect the two sides back together with your nails.
- Place the lemon in the jar.
- Pour vinegar into the jar, leaving and inch at the top.
- Optionally you can add:

    - A dash of cayenne pepper to give the energy a kick *if* it is imperative it happens quickly. Otherwise always choose patience!
    - The juice of a lime
    - Whisky, rum, or other 80 proof alcohol, but remember these do not freeze.
    - Cloves to dominate the situation
    - Onion to completely cut off a relationship
    - Salt for cleansing
    - Bee or Wasp for stinging punishment
    - Ants for constant small annoyances that build up and eat away slowly.
    - Dirt from the home, workplace, school, etc of the target to target them more specifically.
    - Graveyard dirt for death or total destruction. Always ask the spirits before using their dirt and preferably use that of your family if possible. Always leave an offering when entering or leaving a burial site for spiritual purpose.
    - Broken glass, nails, needles etc to add sharp disappointment and cutting words.
    - Anything else you can think of to add symbolically for your well being and success.
- Put the jar on a plate, pie dish or tray, and light a wax candle on top, allowing the wax to flow down the sides of the jar.
- Pray and sing as you watch it burn, and you can even decorate the plate with lemons, limes and some items left over that didn't make it in the jar, but *be careful* with the sharp objects and make sure this plate stays safe.
- When the candle is done (depends on how large yours was), you can leave this in a special space where you will see it daily.
- For 1-4 weeks shake the jar and/or light candles over the jar daily. Pray over it. Pay attention to it. Don't forget about it, especially if you really need results ASAP.

- When you are satisfied that the target's life has begun to crumble or you intuitively trust it is time, you can choose to put the jar in a paper bag and into your freezer to freeze them in a state of destruction, decay, and chaos.
- Keep the jar frozen forever, or for as long as you deem necessary. If you are ready to stop this Work's effects, allow it to thaw and bury the jar, sprinkling salt on the lid and around the jar before you cover.

*If you think your Work has backfired, do a cleansing bath with hyssop or alternative cleansing herb. Go to the crossroads and bury your jar, leaving an offering of honey for your Ancestors when you are done. Pray and talk with your Ancestors about the situation.

Notes:

“Blood of My Womb” Reconnection Ritual

When you come to understand the precious power that comes with your moon cycle, as well as how it affects you, it becomes less of an overall burden, and can even become a personal way to add extra energy and vitality to your personal, spiritual rootwork.

Many shy away from doing any sort of blood magic, and this is totally understandable. If you are interested in utilizing some of your most powerful personal blood for manifestation and creative purposes, however, read further and see if you can tweak this Work for yourself.

Need:

- Small collection of flowers, leaves, and twigs from outside to represent Earth. Read the energy of each plant before choosing it. Ask it if you can use it for your womb healing and pay attention to the feeling you have afterwards. If it is negative, move on until you feel particularly called by a plant's energy.
- A fan, or incense/smoke cleansing herbs to represent Air. Fan's are easy because you can simply fold a piece of pretty paper accordion style to create a nice one.
- Fire can be represented with a candle or an oil lamp, which our Ancestors used and are generally considered safer than wax candles.
- The dark liquid above is represents blood, though this is not always feasible. If you menstruate, it is a simple matter of utilizing a menstrual cup, or even "free bleeding" for a short time into a cup to collect what is considered one of the more powerful sources of Ashe/DNA in rootwork. If you do not do so predictably, you might consider alternatives.

  Depending on your cycle or needs, it may not be convenient (especially if working with a time constraint), practical, or comfortable for you. Appropriate alternatives include wine, blessing water, or spring or rain water. You can also create a lovely reddish liquid with rose petals in water (or rose petal powder, if you have it).
- A small potted plant or a bowl filled with earth. This is to pour your libations into. You could do this in your backyard or outside on private property and use the ground below you feet as "earth".
- A bell. (or some other instrument… You can also clap, knock or stomp.)
- Optional: Make a playlist that speaks to you emotionally & spiritually about where your womb is at/where you want it to be. Play the songs when you spend time at your altar so they are associated with time you spend reconnecting with your womb. Create a stomping rhythm that goes with your music and dance until exhausted periodically,

reconnecting with your body and womb without long periods of neglect, or constant ritual.

Ritual:

- In front of your altar of choice (Ancestor, Womb, Dreams/Personal, Religious/Deity Centered, Cultural, Sexual, etc depending on your practice and your needs)
- Use blessing oil/water to anoint your forehead, heart, and womb and say, *"I am that I am, a shining being walking in the light of my Ancestors."*
- Ring your bell or stomp/clap/knock 3x.
- Say, "*I call to the Ancestors, both known and unknown. The matrilineal, the feminine, and the healers. Those who understood the creative power of the womb and the wild soul. I need you at this time.*" Give a genuine prayer to them. Ask them to come aid your connectivity with your womb center. Let them know your are humbly seeking guidance from those you trust the most. Ask for the intuition to understand the signs as they are given to you.
- Dress your candle with a Condition Oil *or* pour your Condition Oil in the oil lamp while praying. Light it.
- Arrange the plants into a womb shape by the dim light.
    - As you arrange and continue this ritual, feel free to sing/chant the words, *"My womb is my altar; I love and honor this"*.
- At the bottom left, place the cup of blood, wine, or water.
- At the bottom right, place the fan.
- Breath deeply and center your mind on your womb and the power that is in there. Hold your hands to your womb space and imagine the power within growing hotter and brighter beneath your palms. See it as it oozes out and surrounds your body as a shield. See it expand around you and form a covering of protection, love, and security. See it act as a shield of strength for your body and soul.
- Pick up the cup of blood and hold it high. Chant:

"With this blood from sacred space
Ancient power, strength and grace.
The wisdom to know what to keep.
And what's not serving be released

Maiden, mother, and the crone:

Ancestral guides; I'm not alone

My womb is connected with me...

My body and spirit forever free.

- Pour the blood into the Earth. When you have poured the last of your menses into the soil, allow the wild one to be released from your soul and presented before the altar. Who would you be if you weren't concerned what others think? Be that person now, totally comfortable. Open the gates, untether them….however you lock up your "wildish criatura", release it now.
    - Unleash and show this inner wild one through smoking (cigars and herbal blends), playing music, singing, or wild dancing around the altar. Unleash this spirit through yoga, freestyle, hooping, or chanting. **Find the way that expressed wildness and freedom while still being true to you.**
- Finish the session by lying quietly on your back, breathing even and deep, with both hands on your womb space creating a triangle. Meditate and rest with your womb for at least 10 minutes.
- Take the items that can be kept and place them on or around your altar. The flowers can be given back to the Earth the next day.
- To keep your womb altar up, place 9 glasses of water in the same shape as the flowers above. You can keep fresh flowers and other decor on this womb altar, but the water serves as a portal to your Ancestors and the Spirit Realm. More on this in the "Ancestor Altar" section, later in the book.
- If you don't have room for yet another altar, or wish to make your womb altar much more personal, try the old hoodoo tradition of a Mojo

Bag (a similar concept called a "satchel" by Wiccans and other pagans). Place miniature symbols, slips of paper, small amounts of dirt, dry foods, bones, shells, seeds, pictures, and other offerings into a small drawstring bag (that once closed goes unopened). This allows for a personal, portable sacred space to concentrate on and pour your energy into. Try using small pill capsules to fill with the elements. Cleanse the items with saltwater before placing inside.

Notes:

Part Four: Postpartum Rituals

Honey Pot Chronicles #4

Inwardly I zone myself. It is time to.
They say the only way to get things done
is to run solo and see the job through
and I have been known
to call on my inner strength
and do the impossible.
At times it has appeared there is no way,
that my limbs are too beat to move,
but I know me better than anyone.
I don't break.
Even in the strongest of winds I bend,
because at the lowest points of my life,
all I had was my spirit,
easing my tired body along.
And as I rise with myself
and my bloodline
I cannot help
but be ready for my own future.

I have my vision.
I am powerful enough to maintain it.
No obstacles can stop me in this...
This is beyond intentions--
this is fat, and have I mentioned
Fire, Water, Crystals, Air,
Earth, Ether, Ashe, Hair,
Conjure Woman, Brujeria,
Indigenous Healing--
Mother Earth!
I work roots of old--
My inner beast
does not fear to exist.

Postpartum is a word that refers to the time after the delivery of a child from the womb. Usually people only think about the postpartum period if a child (or baby bump) is visible.

The thing is, the body starts changing even in the first few weeks of pregnancy. The body, mind, and spirit changes as new paths open before you both rationally and irrationally. Wombs are born with millions of eggs, and the process of creation and death are a part of the cycles that comes with its inner power. This is nothing to fear, despise, or be shocked by.

Many today are coming to understand what our Ancestors long have known--that honoring all of the transitions in life is important...even the tragic ones that break your heart. Normalizing the event and the celebration and/or healing that follows helps the community rebuild and peace to be rebuilt.

As you partake in, host, and witness these events, look for opportunities to include children in your ceremonies. Make them feel welcome whether they are yours, your clients, part of the family, close friends, or merely a part of the neighborhood.

"In Power. In Balance."
Abortion Healing Altar

This might seem a strange way to some, to start a postpartum section with what is a forceful entrance into a "postpartum" period. I hope to change some of the stigma regarding that.

As long as wombs have been getting pregnant, womb bearers have been aborting the fetuses. Emmenagogues such as Pennyroyal, and even hangers and other items have long been used as abortifacients for desperate people. Thankfully, today's medical abortions are much safer than the risky herbal and physical remedies of the past, which have taken many lives.

Your body is yours and there's no reason to feel guilty about it...and yet that's exactly how many people would have people with womb's feel about making personal choices with it about birth and child rearing. But pregnancy changes the body, mind, and spirit. Birth does too. And that doesn't mention the lifetime commitment to a child. These are personal decisions to make with your own body--no one else's.

Anyone who has had one knows there are so many mixed feelings that arise after an abortion. Between what people are telling you that you should feel, what your body is physically going through, and what your mind and heart say it can be difficult to find appropriate closure for this event. Occasionally some people develop Post Abortion Stress Syndrome. Many do not realize they need support and so do not seek it.

Even when you feel completely fine after an abortion, it is still important to take the time to honor your womb after an important decision and rite of passage that not every person with a womb takes.

Honoring the spirit that was once within you is respectful not only to the Ancestors, but to yourself. Acknowledging your womb and the journey the two of you take together is imperative to continued spiritual growth and clarity on your womb healing journey.

<u>Ritual</u>:

- Find a quiet space and a moment alone somewhere private that you can make a small, hidden altar and spend some time.
- Using the picture at the beginning for reference, make your altar. *Pray over each piece before you lay it down. Ask for healing.* Make it unique according to the circumstances you see. Look for where the altar wants to be made.
    - Use string, tape, sand, or what you have, make a symbol in the ground that represents comfort, family, or healing to you.
    - Use feathers to represent the lightness of your heart that you need.
    - Seashells represent purity, wisdom, and the healing of water and salt. They also are symbolic of a prosperous journey.
    - In the center of the display, place a leaf and a nut (to be used symbolically).
        - The leaf represents hope, revival, fertility, and growth. It is symbolic of new beginnings.
        - The nut is representative of perseverance and tenacity--endurance through hardship. It represents a breakthrough. Remember that the best part of the but is inside of the tough exterior. The nut is also symbolic of the

Egyptian Goddess Nut, the womb and sky mother. She represents both resurrection and rebirth.

- Spend time praying and meditating at the altar. Call to your Ancestors to comfort you. Breath deeply the fresh air for as long as you can.
- If you have not yet named the child, do so now. Not necessarily because you wanted to have this child, even, but so you can refer to terms that aren't "the abortion".
- Write a letter to yourself in the following space. *Write down whatever it is you need to hear*--whatever positive thing you have heard or wish you heard from others (including the child in your womb if you need to). Forgive yourself, congratulate yourself, walk yourself through it, whatever. Attach more paper if necessary.

- Read your letter out loud to yourself. Believe every word of it.
- Leave the altar, walk away, and don't look back.

Notes:

"Release and Regain"
Miscarriage Meditation

Miscarriage is a grief and fear you carry around silently within your heart. No one sees what once was … few know and fewer care. When people do talk about miscarriage, the words are cold, cruel, and noncommittal.

"It wasn't a real child yet." (But it was to you.)

"You can just try again!" (Dismisses your grief as invalid).

"Maybe the child would be ." (As though there's ever a reason you'd be wrong to want your child.)

"At least your womb works." (That has nothing to do with the loss…)

1 in 5 people who have the ability to get pregnant have experienced a miscarriage. Many people don't realize they have had one, and believe it is simply a heavier period. The only way to know for sure is through fertility charting or a pregnancy test.

Miscarriages happen. It doesn't mean anything is wrong with you. We are born with 2 million eggs….but this doesn't mean each one will (or should) become a live human.

Physically the body heals quickly after a miscarriage--usually within 2-4 weeks. Spiritually, the loss can take more time...no one forgets a miscarriage. This meditation encourages you to release the pain, but also symbolically encourages fertility.

- *Set the mood for yourself in your room or somewhere else private, yet comfortable, where you can lay down and watch the candles next to you. Play music softly, but keep it to spa and meditative sounds that do not distract from your peaceful thoughts.*
- *Create a similar small altar with an egg (preferably fertile) in the center. The four candles represent the four directions, the leaves are a bed for the egg. Orange is for joy, happiness, wealth, and the release of negativity as you try and uplift.*
- *As you light the candles, offer a prayer to the Ancestors. Ask for healing and support.*
- *Sit yourself comfortably by the altar.*
- *Steady your breathing. Let your mind clear and your heart be open as your deep breaths open your lungs and chest, bringing cleansing air to your entire body.*
- *Slowly relax each cell in your body, inch by inch, starting with your head, neck, and shoulders, and working your way down.*
- *Release the floodgates of your emotions at this time. Allow yourself to feel whatever feelings come--negative and positive. Remember the good times, and the bad. Cherish both as these feelings come and go.*
- *As the grief and the loss covers you, allow yourself to consider how far you've come, what you've learned, and how you've changed and grown in this time.*
- *When the time has come, call to the spirit of your child. If you already have a name for them, use their name. Allow them to come to your arms and be cradled by you.*
- *Imagine your world with your child. Imagine your lifetime together as guardian to their needs and life. Imagine and cherish what could have been.*
- *Embrace your precious baby in your arms. Give them love. Fuss over them the way parents do. Listen to any messages this Ancestor has to say. They will let you know you are forgiven because there is nothing really to forgive. They understand and probably knew what was going to happen long before you did.*

- *Allow your grief to be softened and make peace with your emotions.*
- *When you are ready, bring yourself back to the present time slowly. Remember that visiting with your child--an Ancestor-- is available to you always. This is a special relationship that you have.*

When you are done with your meditation you can choose what to do with your egg. You can take it outside and bury it with prayer, or you can use it in a spiritual bath. For a bath, mix the yolk with 3 more eggs (to represent the 4 seasons), mix with honey in a bowl, and pour it over your head, allowing the yolk to wash over your hair and body. Do not fear the raw yolk--many common hair and skin conditioners and treatments contain egg.

Notes:

"What I Had Was the Earth"
Stillbirth Healing

The grief of a stillbirth is a bit more vocal than a miscarriage. After all, there is a good chance that everything was going fine through the pregnancy, and that you were vocal about your excitement of your future. There is a chance that your stomach was showing signs of pregnancy (after all, this was after 24 weeks) and that people had taken notice, wished you well, and even checked up on you later.

Even with this obvious tragedy, eventually most voices fall silent, and few truly remember. Because of the silence, many who have lost are left alone to struggle. They do not realize they can take pictures, talk, or grieve with the body and soul of their lost child. Many don't even realize both parents are equal as mourners.

A beautiful way to actively mourn and grieve in a positive manner is to take care of a plant, or plant a garden. Caring for something, and watching its subsequent life and growth, is healing.

Gardens and horticulture are known to be healing. Being in a green setting makes the body automatically feel safer and causes dips in cortisol--the stress hormone. Spending time actively in a green space (yours or a communal one) allows you to feel as restful as the flowers and greenery before you look. Every day you have something to look forward to--to note its growth and tend to its needs. You have something you began that is relying on you--something that adds beauty and life to the world around you.

Plants don't comfort you out loud--but they don't judge you either. The physical activity necessary for their care gets your blood moving every day, their cleansing and bright presence and the reward of a job well done is beyond words. Be sure to choose "easy" plants to cultivate, and research on them to set yourself up for success.

<u>Rebirth Garden:</u>

- Choose who you would like to commemorate and celebrate your child. Allow your family to remain as private as you wish with no guilt. Hold space for only those who should have space held.
- Set up the area for planting prior.
- Smoke cleanse the space spiritually.
- Call on the Ancestors, and include the child you are honoring as one of them.
- Recite a poem or sing a song that has special meaning to you. Consider asking a talented friend or family member, or hiring someone to lead this. Sample words:
    - *I whisper your name to the wind.*
      It still belongs to you.
      I feel you beyond me
      Beside me
      Behind me.
      You never leave.
      I whisper your name to the wind

To let you know
I love you.

- Communally plant your seeds. The seeds can be what you would like. A tree. A bush. Flowers. A vegetable garden. Choosing seeds and helping them grow is a healing act for yourself and the planet.
- If you have the placenta, you might consider another private ceremony where you bury it, or release it down the river.

*Do not rush yourself or your ritual. Give yourself time to get to a place of willingness to do a healing ritual such as this.

Write any notes and thoughts you have before or after this ritual:

"Down by the Altar"
Loss of a Child

Losing a loved one is hard, but the loss of a child is a tragedy beyond words. The devastation of knowing them, loving them, raising them, and losing them, no matter for how long or little time, simply cannot be put into words or measured. Around you the world forgets, but you are left with memories of not only what was, but what could have been.

One of the most healing steps you can take to ritualistically mourn your loss is to add your child to the Ancestor altar where they belong. Again, both parents should be treated as mourners.

Ancestor Altar

An Ancestor altar is a way to dedicate a part of your living space to those who came before you. All black people should have an altar up to communicate with their Ancestors, regardless of the deity they serve. This is *very* important for spiritual and physical world health. This is a place you will meditate, dwell on, and also speak with and work with your Ancestors.

It does not have to be big or extravagant, but having a place of honor for your Ancestors is a beautiful way to remember you are not alone, you do have a purpose, and that you are special wonderfully made. After all, you were once but a dream that someone wished for--an aunt, a grandpa, a parent.

You may come to realize you are comforted by the memories on your altar, that you spend time talking to and remembering those you may have been neglecting.

While altars vary (and you should do and use what you can especially if you have no other options), it is important to have 9 glasses of water on your altar. These will serve as a connection and portal to the Spiritual Realm from here on Earth. Communication is the main essence of this altar (not just as a place of memories). Get creative and make use of face jugs, copper cups, or shot glasses, to fit your own needs and desires for your altar space.

Hang pictures of your Ancestors (no one living) on the wall around your mirror (if it's on the wall) above the altar. Also have candles or your oil lamp on the altar for Work and a mirror should be there as well. Fresh flowers or potted plants are also often included.

Every Monday, change your water and flowers, wipe off dust, smoke cleanse, and set offerings. Offer prayer and don’t forget to listen to what is said in return. Do a divination method-- use a pendulum, throwing bones, tarot, etc-- and really read your own body and wellness, as well as your whole home.

Though not necessary, many people prefer also placing representation of their Ancestors as a form of memorialization. This could be pictures, ashes, old journals, a lock of hair, a family tree, or a keepsake from the family member.

Ancestors are people of your bloodline, but the ones celebrated on this altar should be ones you trust in your home and heart. Ancestors can even be famous people from your culture or community, and these can be represented by pictures, literature, sheet music, and more.

Plants, mirrors, crystals and flowers all add different benefit to your altar, but remember there is no need to go overboard.

Purchase a bottle of one of your ancestor's favorite liquor, and occasionally pour them a shot. Bring them the cigar they used to smoke, or a shell you know they would have enjoyed. Light incense and smoke cleanse. When you cook something good, share it. Cook just for them sometimes.

When you pass the altar, say hello. When you are feeling depressed and lonely, pull up a chair and rest. When you pray, sit by your family. You are not alone. They love, forgive, and cherish you always.

Meditate and then list personal items that should be on your Ancestor altar:

"Lay Hands & Pray"
A Postpartum Ceremony

Around the world, postpartum rituals are abound. Even in the most secluded places, those who give birth (and the community around them) find similar ways to honor the life giving portal. Many include forms of binding the belly and body of the mother, adorning them with new jewelry, symbols, or attire. Each ceremony finds a personal and loving way to honor this journey and right of passage as a person who has just ushered another human into this world. These ceremonies are also a form of celebration, as well as a moment in between this realm, and that of our spirit guides and Ancestors.

Below I have written a spiritual postpartum ritual to guide you on your path to creating your own personal ceremony. Find what works for you, and keep your intuitive minds eye open to alternatives that you can utilize in your own personal situation. Always speak from the heart during the ceremony if you can. If you are a spiritual guide who wishes to do these types of ceremonies for rituals with those in your community, I advise you to practice on family or friends that you love and trust.

Feel free to change suggestions, words and phrases to use the following ceremony to honor those in your life whose wombs need ritual healing after stillbirth, miscarriage, loss, or abortion, as well as those of specific sexualities and life experiences. Postpartum ceremonies bring closure and wellness to many situations and are not only limited to people celebrating the birth of a child and new mom.

Step 1: Preparation

Your ceremony should begin with you preparing the area.

- An altar should be erected. It should be womb, mother, and life centered in nature. Flowers/leaves, statues, beads, lights, and more can all be used. Make this part personal and special to you
- Other decor can include candles, relaxing or traditional scents (if the mother allows it), incense, and calm music (such as the pan drum or flutes) can all create a peaceful and loving atmosphere.
- Set your ritual items up, so they are accessible. Lay seven scarves (around 1.5 yards long to go around the widest part of the body) horizontally down the floor, in line with each other with each other.

Draw and color your ideal altar for birth ceremonies:

Step 2: Spiritual Bath

Depending on when the ceremony takes place, a Spiritual Bath is the best first course of action. Only do a bath after the new parent has healed completely from birth. This is typically 2-4 weeks postpartum.

Baths are preferable, due to the healing and relaxing nature of bathing, however a shower can also suffice if necessary, keeping the ceremony quick, though preferably there will be a small stool for the recipient to sit on.

- Smoke cleanse the bathroom and entire house with a smoke cleansing stick, or incense and herbs in a bowl.
- Fill the tub with steaming hot water.
- As it fills, add half a cup of sea salt.
- Add 1 large pot of herbal water that has been steeped overnight (or at least 5 hours….Boil the water first, then place the herbs inside, cover, take off heat, and allow to sit). *The water should be dark with the herbs.* Use what you have or are able to buy. Learn of any roots and herbs that you know are used for postpartum and write note of them for your own special blend. Below are some suggestions.

    - Turmeric, bay leaves, ginger root, and star anise will all add a rich scent as well as their own healing properties, both for the skin as well as circulation and digestion.
    - Red raspberry leaf, oat straw, catnip, and shepherds purse are all healers commonly used during postpartum for gentle, yet effective womb healing.
    - Rose petals, calendula, chamomile and lavender are all perfect for beautification and a sweet demeanor.
    - Myrrh, comfrey, sage, and sea salt are all common postpartum natural healers used worldwide.
    - Include the leaves and sticks from the herbs in the bath! (If you are giving the bath to a new mom, be sure you are the one to clean it up, or just use teabags/a mesh teaball).
- Light candles around the room, and play soft music with a pleasant melody (no ambient sounds, or anything too simple).
- When the tub is full, add 2-3 drops of an essential oil, such as lavender, peppermint, cinnamon, or citrus.
- On top of the water, spread a layer of fresh flower petals, preferably ones that are large and thick for easy clean up. Feel free to include leaves. Go over the top with a 2nd, contrasting color petal and draw a design on the top. This can be as simple as a circle, to as complex as an initial or symbol. (Gently rinse off the petals before adding. *Be sure not to add anything poisonous!* Gathering is great, but do your research beforehand.)
- Lead the postpartum person you are honoring to the bath. Help them undress, and have them stand before the tub.
- Smoke cleanse around the honoree, praying to the Ancestors:
    - *"We pray in honor of Sankofa, and we offer praise for our lives today.*
    - *We give praise to ___________ (honoree's name), who has undertaken the journey of childbirth and courageously pushed through the struggles.*

    - *We give praise to the struggles that came before them, those of other births and other parents in the family. We witness the struggle of the bloodline throughout history.*
    - *We give praise to the Elders, who keep tradition and pass it on.*
    - *We give praise to those who love, support, and care for ___________. Thank you for all that you do.*
    - *We give praise to Asase Yaa/Mother Earth for providing us a world with which to not only sustain ourselves, but teach ourselves.*
    - *We give praise to the Ancestors, strong and wise. Guide ___________ on their journey towards knowledge, growth and clarity.*
    - *Ashe! Ashe! Ashe!*
- Help the honoree into the hot water and into a seated position.
- Give them a chance to soak in the tub.
- Invite the honoree to address any aspects of the birth, new parenthood and their role that they may want to talk about, resolve, and pray over.
- Take fistfuls of the herbs and petals and scrub their body with the plants, chanting:
  You are blessed, cherished, and protected.
- Have every womb bearer and/or specially chosen people in the home who wish to offer the honored birther wellness, health, wisdom, and prosperity come in one at a time to take the herbs and wash the honoree's body as well. This ensures that all of the babies in the family and community will receive these blessings as well.
  (This will hopefully be a private affair, but in case there are questionable family or friends at the home, have a spiritual guide there to read everyone (with pendulum or otherwise) before they enter into the home/hall to be given a chance to give a blessing).
- Continue the chanting, having someone clap or play an instrument to keep time.
- When the last person has scrubbed the honoree with herbs, all those present can sway in unison with hands held over them. Whoever is

leading the ceremony will pray and those swaying respond "Ase" to each blessing that is called forth powerfully and assertively:

   - *To our kindred ___________ ,*
   - *May the blessing of the Spirit be upon you.*
   - *May the Ancestors help you for the sake of your devotion and well being.*
   - *May what the Ancestors knew, become what you know.*
   - *May you be your best self.*
   - *May you walk with confidence because of your power.*
   - *May you be protected in this new endeavor.*
   - *May you walk in beauty with every step you take.*
   - *May you be honorably greeted when you arrive.*
   - *May your guides be with you at every crossroads.*
   - *Ase.*

- Allow them to rise from the heat of the water, and dry off with towels (hopefully warmed!). Be sure to offer a refreshing glass of water with lemon for hydration, but do not include ice.

Write or draw any notes or ideas you may have:

Step 3: Light Oil Massage

Take an infused oil (infused in the same way as a tincture with pregnancy and breastfeeding safe, soothing herbs). Rub the entire body down with oil, massaging and pampering. Give special attention to the womb, being gentle, yet firm.

Take your time with the massage.

Be sure to bless and infuse the oil prior to the ceremony. The same as your other jars and rootwork rituals, take time with the oil. Allow it to infuse as long as you can. Keep it buried, or let it soak in the sun or moon rays. Pray with it. Talk with the Ancestors. Focus on the energy being a healing one for birth, fertility, wombs, family, and wellness.

Notes:

Step 4: Adinkra Symbol

Using Jagua or Henna, whichever your preference, choose an Adinkra symbol to adorn the honoree's body, right between the rib cage. Be sure to wipe the area clean with a wet, then dry cloth for the longest stain. Jagua is made from a dark berry and will dye the skin close to black...you will note that it dries clear and the color comes in hours later. Henna tends to dry more on the orange and brown side for darker skin tones, getting darker under the application the longer it is left.

Created in what is today referred to as Ghana, Adinkra symbols were named after the King of the Gyaaman Kingdom, who surrendered for peace after a war with the Ashanti people over his own use of their sacred Golden Stool symbol. The knowledge of the symbols was passed on through the cloth he had wrapped himself in during his final moments, decorated in the symbols of his people, and became common use among the Ashanti people. Each Adinkra symbol has its own meaning, with power of its own, there from generations of use and repetition. Therefore, it is best to choose this symbol long before the ceremony even begins...speak with the honored parent to understand their needs and which will most benefit them by being marked on their body.

In the picture at the beginning of this section, the symbol of *Sankofa* is simply placed on the body between the breasts. More than one symbol can be added, and remember they do not have to be Adinkra, and can be any traditional symbols from Africa or the Diaspora that you desire. According to skill level, this can be done ornately, or with what you have. You might find it easier to use tools in henna kits, or to simply use a paintbrush.

These dyes last 2+ weeks, depending on how deep you let the stain get.

Sketch Your Favorite Symbols Below:

Step 5: Bone Closing

From Morocco to Mexico, bone closing has been practiced by thousands of indigenous and tribal birthers and birth workers for centuries. Some societies perform a bone closing on Day 3 postpartum, others on Day 40, and still others do it weekly for 3-4 months (commonly called the 4th trimester).

There are many ways to do a bone closing, but generally this is done by swaddling/enclosing the postpartum person in cloth from head to toe. Beginning at the head, two people work all the way down to the feet.

The purpose of Bone Closing is two-fold; physical and spiritual.

The act of bone closing encourages the bones, inner organs, and muscles (most importantly the womb) back into place, as well as applies pressure to swelling. The practice is yet another that reminds us to keep the womb warm, as a cotton cocoon will do just that to a wrapped body.

Spiritually, the body is closed after the very “opening” act of birth. Many cultures believe a birther leaves their body spiritually to retrieve the child’s soul from the Ether or Spirit Realm. Others say the “opening” for growth begins much sooner, back in pregnancy. This ceremony closes this portal.

Some people include the newborn in the ceremony by having the honoree hold them on their chest. Others keep this ceremony strictly for honoring the birther. Many small choices can make the ceremony personal, from incorporation of music, sound therapy, aromatherapy, prayer, and more.

Notes:

General Ceremony:

- You can choose to use 9 cloths *or* use one and slide it down (beneath) the body from head to toe, stopping 9 times (some do this with the same cloth they will use to bind the belly later….traditional birthworkers have been known to use the shawl from around their shoulders or waist….some modern women create their own set of scarves or cloths).
    - The 9 strips of cloth should be long enough to wrap around most postpartum bodies. Be certain the fabric is long enough before beginning the ceremony. Typically this will be 6-9 inches wide and 1.5-2 yards (6 feet) long.
    - The fabric can be your choice. Some choose traditional fabric from their community, others choose something fancy, symbolic or beautiful that speaks to them. Others choose fabric with specific symbols or colors. You might choose to use the 7 colors of the rainbow, and include 2 additional strips in black and white, 9 colors with meaning to you (and write a poem or story for each), or choose cloth with a specific pattern or meaning. Whatever fabric you choose to make your bone closing kit with, make it special, unique and sacred to you.

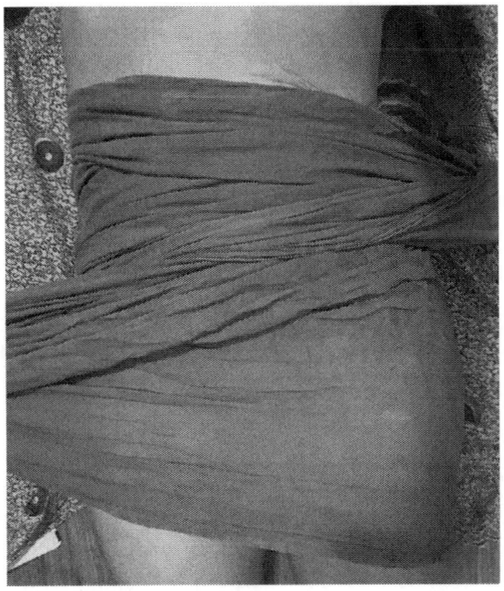

- Lay the long strip(s) flat on the floor.
- Have the honoree lay on the strip(s) with their head on a small pillow.
- Light a candle at their head and feet (within safe distance.

- Seat one person on either side of the honoree. You can use more people if you have a larger group who wishes to bless and lay hands on the postpartum person. 3-6 people on either side usually is the limit for being seated comfortably, so choose beforehand. The person leading the ceremony should be one of them.
- Beginning with the head, take one side of the fabric and pass it to the person on the opposite side. Take the other and do the same.
- Using the fabric, "hug" the body by each side gently, but firmly pulling on their side of the fabric to bring the body "closed".
- As you move down the body, shake, rock, turn to the sides, and rhythmically move as you all feel called. This may require prior practice.
- If using *multiple strips of fabric*, tie the fabric in place *once* firmly (on the head cover the eyes, but leave the mouth and nose in the air for breathing). There is no need to completely knot in place.
    - You can also simply hand each end to a person on either side and have them hold the fabric firmly in hand until the, knotting only at the finish, one at a time.
- If using *one strip of fabric*, simply slide the wrap down a few inches and repeat the hugging and shaking with the cloth.
- Continue the "closing" process until you reach the feet.
- Turn music on and leave the honoree to rest and consider the experience. If you used 9 separate scarfs/strips of cloth, they will be all swaddled up at this point.
    - This can take 15-45 minutes as needed.

After the Bone Closing the womb can be massaged again lightly, and the belly bound.
Bone Closing, though typically only used postpartum after childbirth or child loss, has been known to be incorporated into other rituals for large events that need great healing, such as a returned soldier from war or a great achievement.

Notes:

Step 6: Hot Stone Press

Gather 3 stones with flat surfaces on at least one side from your neighborhood. They should be 3 different sizes, and should be able to sit together in a small pot or slow cooker to heat up when prepared.

Using acrylic paint, permanent markers, crochet, gold leaf, and any other (flat!) decor that you feel truly represents you, decorate the 3 stones with images and symbols which are powerful to you. Using white paint creatively on a gray or black canvas can yield beautiful results that symbolically represents balance in all things--an ancient Indigenous practice worldwide. Painting simple ovals and creating faces on them to represent the Ancestors, your deity or spirits, or the ritual masks of times passed can also be a very effective way to connect the stones to your personal practice. Names, short blessings or prayers, Adinkra symbols, eyes, animals, flowers and leaves….Mother, Maiden, Crone...Sun, Moon, and Stars….whatever truly speaks to your practice and nature, whatever it is that calls to you, draw it there. Make these three stones truly your own. These are healing stones, and what you draw on them are healing images, imbued with your energy. Channel them with love, strength, and Ancestral spirit.

<u>In a square cloth, put equal parts of the following powdered herbs</u>:

- Black Pepper
- Cumin
- Cardamom
- Ginger
- Nutmeg
- Cinnamon
- Turmeric
- Anise

These herbs and spices stimulate circulation and aid digestion. They are commonly called "warming herbs" and are used throughout the Eastern world for postpartum and healing remedies. You should also feel free to add your own special and personal touches, such as healing salts, coffee, or other herbs you have researched and feel are beneficial.

Take one of the rocks and place the flat edge in the herbs on the handkerchief. Wrap it up, pulling all excess fabric to the top, and tie it up there as close to the rock as possible with a string or ribbon. Use 9 knots or ribbons to symbolize the Ancestors. Do the same with the other two rocks.

Heating a small crock pot to its lowest temperature, place the three wrapped stones at the bottom of the pot and allow them to warm.

Moisturize the stomach of the honoree lightly with oils from the massage if it appears to have become dry. Using the warmed stones (check the temp on the back of your hand before applying to a sensitive postpartum stomach), begin smoothing the stomach in small circle motions upward, using firm pressure.

The herbs are likely to leave a small amount of residue the skin. Be careful as the tumeric and other herbs can stain clothes. You can wipe this off when done, or (if you prefer to leave them on the skin) place a small cotton cloth on the stomach to cover them before putting a shirt/tank top on.

Notes:

Step 7: Belly Binding

Binding the belly is a sacred womb ritual that dates back for centuries in many indigenous cultures worldwide. The act of taking a long piece of fabric, usually traditionally dyed into vibrant colors, and winding it around the body holds many spiritual and physical benefits for the womb in throughout life's stages.

Traditionally this practice was used most commonly for womb bearers immediately postpartum, in the three months referred to as the “fourth trimester”. During this time, the womb bearer was kept indoors and usually in bed, being fed warm, rejuvenating foods, and spending time bonding with their new child, as well as healing.

Their belly and hips were bound almost continuously to bring the womb back into alignment and close the abdominal muscles and hip bones. It gave the belly and spine support to keep posture upright as the body healed--a necessity while avoiding the breastfeeding slouch.

Within the community, the bright fabric worn over a loose shift dress was a symbol of this right of passage this person had undertook, and was something to be respected. Depending on community, tribe or customs, the very fabric chosen to make it could hold spiritual or familial value to the wearer.

Today more uses are found for this ancient custom, particularly for the healing from miscarriage, stillbirth, diastasis recti and abortion. This is a thoughtful gift for a grieving, or a healing person whose womb might need extra love and care at the moment. It allows for quicker and more comfortable recovery, including lessened bleeding times and a full return of the womb back into position.

Still others find relief from PMS symptoms such as cramps and bloating from a light bind around their midsection. Again this simple ritual of spending time paying attention to the body and soul daily is something many modern women enjoy returning to.

One well made belly binding wrap in a community is a revolution...with it, countless families can share and bind each other. It can be passed down, womb to womb within a family, a symbol of honor as each new member undertakes their rite of passage.

Whether you are postpartum, recovering, or simply menstruating, the act of belly binding is a healing ritual that gives you at least a couple minutes to focus in on yourself, your own body, your own womb, your own feelings, and your own needs. It is symbolic of the journey through life with the power of the womb within your root chakra space.

Making a Belly Binding Wrap:

1. You will need a serger machine, traditional fabric (dyed so it is 2 sided, i.e. batik, ankara, etc), and a soft body ruler.
2. Determine if you will need 2, 2.5, or 3 yards of fabric. Each yard is 3 feet long, and we will cut it into 4 pieces, which means 1 yard will be 12 feet long (most people who wear a size medium will need 24 feet of fabric to effectively bind).

   Sizing:

   a. if you buy 2 yards, your fabric will be 6 feet long. Once we cut it all in 4 pieces and see them together, the wrap will be 24 feet long. This is the perfect length for most people size medium and smaller. In almost every picture you see of me, I am wearing this size.
   b. It is best to purchase 2.5 yards of fabric if you are tall or heavier set. This way you can assure that you will be able to cover your entire torso.
   c. 3 yards of fabric will give you a wrap that is 36ft. I would recommend this size if you are larger than a 2x.
   d. If you are using your belly binding wrap for **waist training purposes** you need to size up! It is better to have a longer one so that you can bind the majority of your core. Add at least half a yard to whatever size you have determined for yourself. Add in increments of half a yard as needed.

3. Take your fabric and spread it wide and flat.

4. Fold it in half, longways.

5. And fold it in half one more time. You should have 4 layers of fabric on top of each other.

6. Cut along each side carefully, so that you have four long strips of equal length.

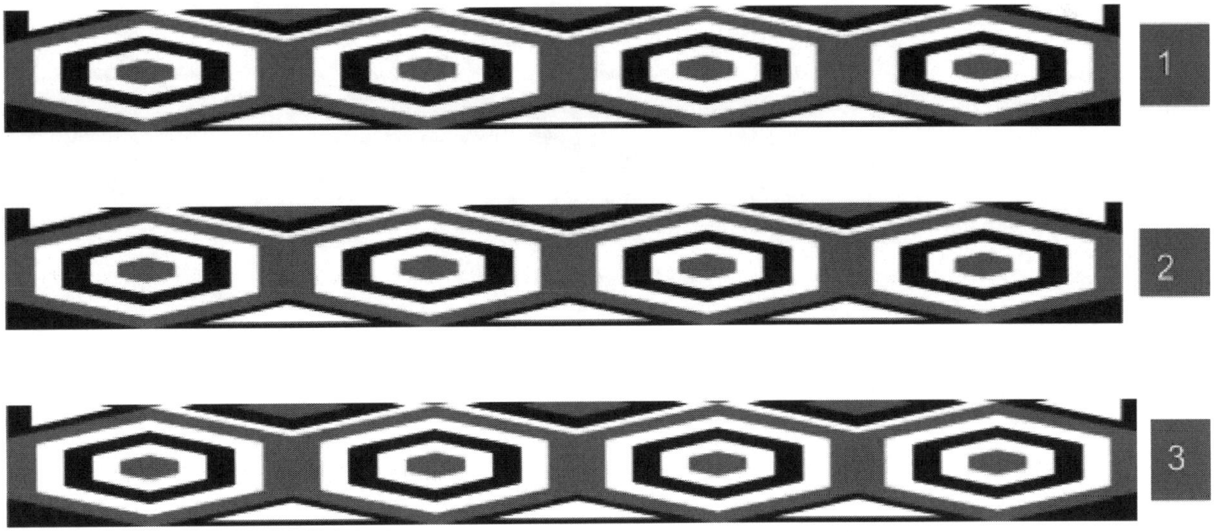

7. Try to find the "right" side of the fabric. With some patterns, this is easier to do, with others it can feel impossible. The "wrong" side will be lighter in color, and might have less dye saturated on it. This side looks a little more faded.
   If you cannot tell the difference between either side of the fabric, don't worry! Just continue on your project. If you can't tell before sewing, you will not be able to tell when the item is worn.
8. Taking care to ensure that the right sides are together, start sewing the strips of fabric together until you have one long strip of fabric.

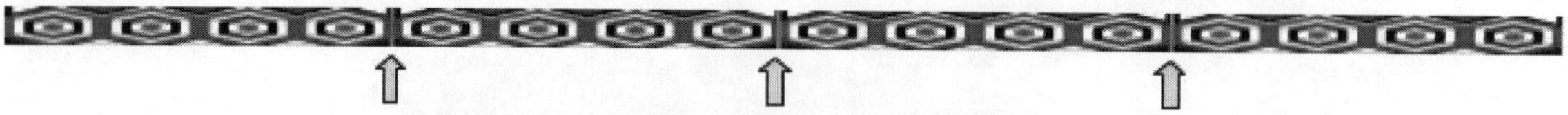

Sew the strips together into one.

9. Serge the outside edges to keep it from fraying. Be sure to keep your lines straight! Depending on your fabric width, your wrap should be between 6-10 inches wide. You can decide if you prefer your strips to be thinner or thicker later, and modify accordingly.

Serge the edges

10. Cut all of the threads and edges off.

You're finished! A simple project and one that will last years to come.

Next are instructions for putting on the wrap yourself. These can be easily modified to help and put the wrap on someone else, however I find that most modern people put on their wrap alone.

How To Put On Your Wrap:

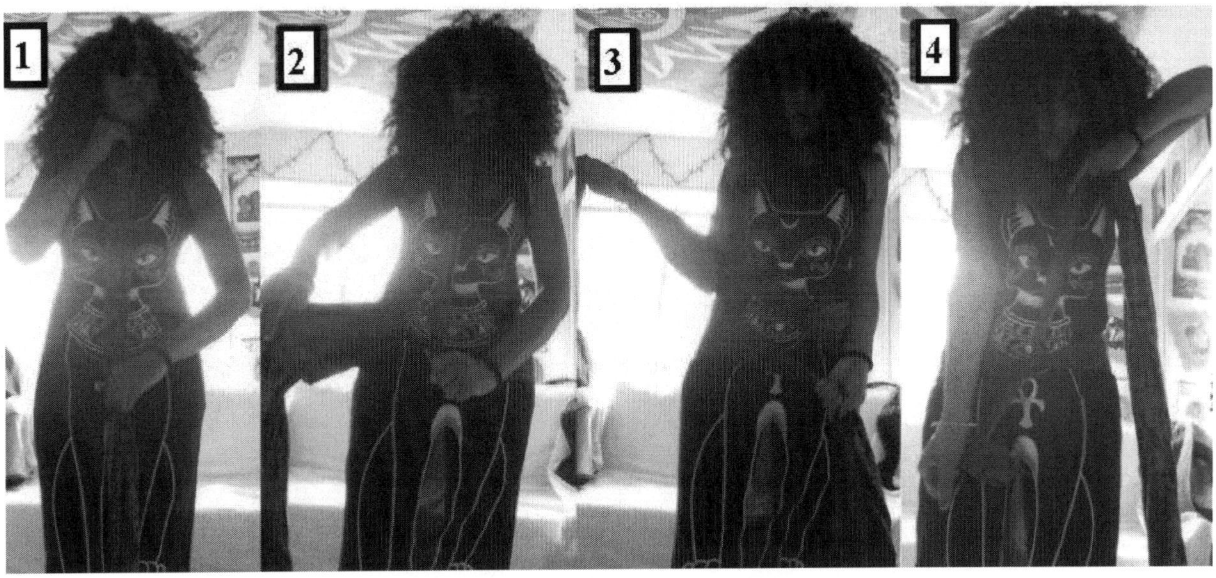

1) Hold one end of the wrap up to your mouth, and the other hand down at the base of your womb. We will call the part above your womb the "short end", and the part below it the "long end".

2) Holding the short end in your mouth, wrap the long end around your body, spreading the wrap flat as wide as possible.

3) Bring the long end under the short end.

4 & 5) Wrap the two ends around each other simultaneously, keeping them both pulled tightly enough for support, but not too tight for comfort.

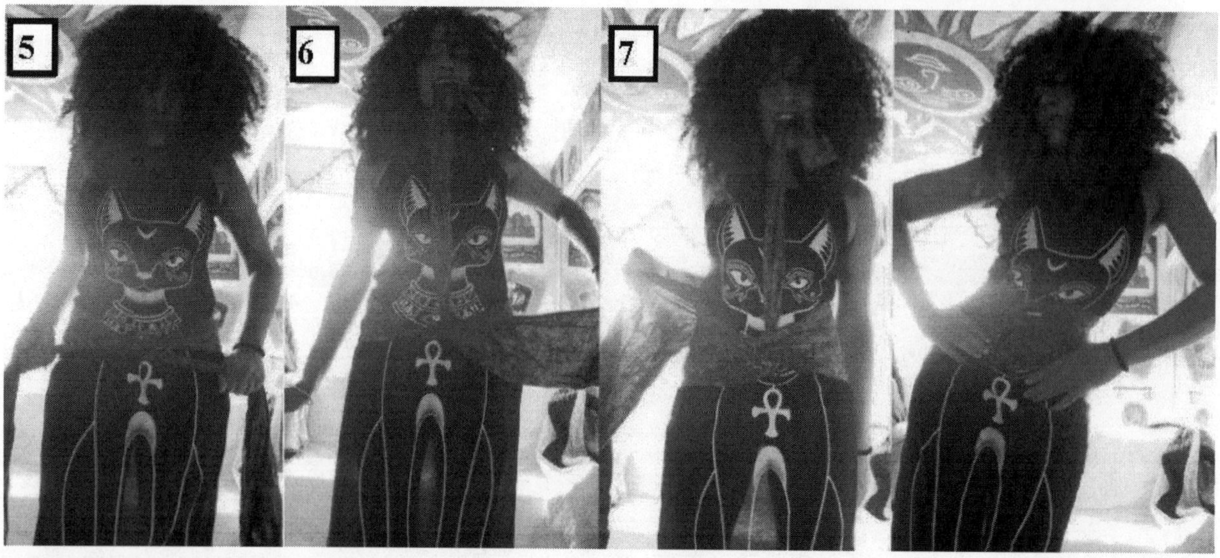

4 & 5) Wrap the two ends around each other simultaneously, keeping them both pulled tightly enough for support, but not too tight for comfort.

6) Bring the short end back up to your mouth. You should have a twisted "knot", and be ready to bring the wrap back around your body again. You will continue wrapping always in the same direction.

7) Continue to wrap your body, being sure to keep the "knots" centered and close to each other to ensure maximum tightness.

8) As you go, you will know you are keeping it tight enough by the pretty pattern the knots begin to make up the front.

9) Tie the two ends together at the top, and tuck in the ends.

<u>Tips For Putting It On:</u>

- Practice, practice, practice! This has a small learning curve, but after a week you will realize you can put it on in minutes.
- Try standing in front of a mirror and watching yourself wrap to be sure it is tight and centered.
- Keep the lowest knot below your womb to be sure you are getting the benefit of womb realignment.
- Only bunch up the fabric at the "knots". When bringing it around your body, keep the fabric as flat as possible!

Notes:

Step 8: After the Ceremony

- Have a flower crown to place on the honoree's head as they feed the baby upon completion of the ritual. Allow this time to be peaceful and private.
- Prepare a delicious and hot tea for to pour at leisure. Leave behind 2-5 bags to be enjoyed later as well!
- Hot soup is an excellent meal to leave behind in a bowl after the ceremony.
- Have guests bring homemade meals to keep in the freezer and fridge of the birther's home.
- Consider bringing a gift for the other children in the home--a video or board game could be considered, or a special trinket for personal spiritual use.

When making this ceremony your own, prepare all the little details in your own way. Learn each time you have completed the ritual, you will learn what works for you and what doesn't, and grow through practice and action.

Mantras for the Newly Postpartum:
Write mantras on notecards, decorate them, and place on the walls around your room or home to remember and feel inspired! Below are some suggestions...choose which apply to you and feel inspired to write your own positive affirmations.

- *I love and accept myself right now in this moment.*
- *I treat myself and my body with respect.*
- *I take my healing and recovery with slow care.*
- *I am steady in my wellness.*
- *I can trust my maternal/parental intuition.*
- *I deserve to do things at the pace of someone who has recently birthed.*
- *My body and being are capable.*
- *I am more than the children my body has birthed.*
- *"A mother's love liberates." – Maya Angelou*
- *I do the best that I can for my children and that is enough.*
- *Being a mother/parent has made me feel beautiful.*
- *My children don't care about my flaws.*
- *I am not alone in how I feel.*
- *The decisions other mothers make do not need to dictate mine.*
- *Nurturing myself is good.*
- *Nurturing myself helps me nurture others.*

- *I accept love and nourishment from the world.*
- *I am flexible in the face of changes.*
- *I am patient with my evolution.*
- *Being a mother/parent comes before whatever I want it to--including housework.*
- *I give myself time to rest and heal.*
- *My Ancestors help guide me as a new parent and guardian.*
- *Being a good parent takes courage. Today I am brave.*
- *I am still myself after motherhood/parenthood.*

Notes:

Birth Reclamation

Many women feel conflicted after the birth of their child. Whether you had a c-section, suffered loss, experienced a rogue doctor, disrespect from family and friends, had an unforeseen illness, an unwanted visitor (or none at all), or had your whole birth plan thrown to the wind, the need to reclaim your personal birth story is not uncommon in the modern birth scene. Between racism and misogyny, many are left with bad memories, feeling lost or robbed, and often left with the bitter thoughts of, "If only I had known…"

One of the main benefits of a yoni egg is that it can re-establish your pelvic strength and overall health after childbirth. Many think that a yoni egg might not be necessary for a postpartum vagina that has not had a vaginal delivery (such as after a c-section or miscarriage). I disagree--in fact, I would like to make the point that a yoni egg (and other tools) can be used for many types of healing! Remember that we can use what we have to really express and release our greatest needs and desires.

Here is a small ritual in which your yoni egg can give you the chance to physically birth where you did not before. Reimagine it and create your own healing rituals as time goes on. Reach within your own heart and outside of your own aura and talk to your Ancestors. Ask them what you need as well.

- The morning of your choosing *at least* 12 weeks postpartum insert your egg with a prayer. Choose a power sentence to say, that begins with "*Today I reclaim*". For example, say, "*Today I reclaim the day I gave birth.*"
- Adorn your body with jewelry such as waistbeads. Wear as many as you can. Add jagua or henna designs to your skin. Do your hair. Wear perfume. Remain nude for as much of the day as you can (if you cannot, wear simple, loose, minimal clothes and forsake underwear to allow your body to breathe and relax. Connect with your inner wild spirit--the primal person within that instinctively knows what to do in and around nature.
- Spend the day feeling powerful and creative, and doing activities that aid you in this. If you cannot find an entire day to do this, find at least some points in which to concentrate on something .
- Occasionally put your hands on your womb and feel the power beneath your fingers. Repeat positive affirmations to yourself such as, "*My womb is an altar of power.*"
- In the evening, prepare a special, sacred bath using salts, herbs, and lots of flowers and leaves (hopefully harvested from the neighborhood).
    - In a large bowl, put the juice of one lemon, 3 drops of mint essential oil, and a splash of vanilla extract. Fill with cold water.
- Soak as long as you would like. Allow the water to envelope your body as a benign, healing, substance.
- Crouch down into a squat as though giving birth (you can put your hands on the ground, your knees on the ground, or however feels most comfortable).
- Using your pelvic muscles (if you don't know how, go back and read the Punanilates section!) and push down with your vagina until you "give birth" to your crystal egg.

- After the birth, take the bowl of cold water, and pour the refreshing mixture over your head, allowing all the invigorating understanding of the power and unique story of your body to wash over you.
- When finished with your bath, go to your room and rub your body down in oils.
- Lay down under the covers, rest and sleep.
- When you wake up, journal your thoughts and feelings.

Try:

*Inviting another person (such as your romantic/sexual partner, especially the one who participated in the birth you are reclaiming) to join you. They can do the ritual with you, or simply aid you and support you during the process.

**Taking a similar bath *with baby safe herbs* later with your baby if you are looking for a bonding exercise. Avoid use of lemon (and many herbs), as these might dry out babies skin. Consider blessing your baby with song and prayer.

Notes:

Part Five: The Path of the Goddess

Honey Pot Chronicles #5

And when I held Knowing in my heart
I could not forget.
It could never again slip my mind that
what I had within was
something special
and all mine.
That I come from such a long, powerful line;
I walk with strength...
"My Ancestors outnumber my fears."

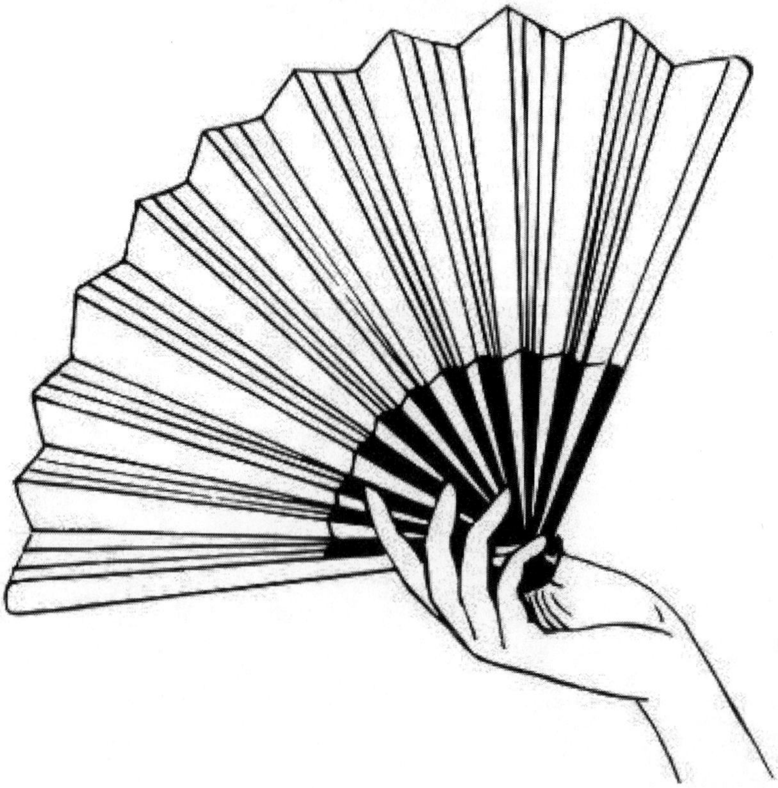

Sacred Sister Circle

The Sacred Sister Circle is a movement to create a sisterhood. Open to Black Women; you can find this safe space at **patreon.com/sacredsistercircle**. This group is for support through your journey with Ancestral Veneration and Rootwork, accompanied by those on similar paths.

Citations

You may notice that I wrote this entire book while barely citing any sources. I did this purposefully.

Part of me believes fully that there is a gift in the act of learning information and doing further research yourself. Do not take my word for anything in this book and do not take it for gospel. Rather, take it and talk with your own Ancestors and spirits. Take this information and speak with your own friends, family, and community. Take it and go read, research, and learn yourself. Nothing written here is a great mystery, though I will admit if you take your questions to the right people, your answers will go deeper than this book could ever hope to hint at.

I also chose not to include instructions to honor the traditions of my indigenous and tribal Ancestors who passed on lore and tales with a great oral tradition. Through word of mouth, from ear to ear, stories spread for centuries and this was The Way. As colonialism halted languages, tore apart tribes, and separated communities, many of these were lost in ways that our Ancestors could not have imagined. In this workbook I return to that way of repeating that which was told to trusted ear and committed to memory. I return to a time when an important story need only be told or heard when necessary, but was beloved and special enough to be passed on forever. I write as I was told and as my brain said the words in my own language. I hope you enjoy returning with me to this practice.

Recommended Shops

These stores are ones that I recommend for perusal during your womb healing journey.

- **Womb Healing Workbooks**: Search "Tahtahme" on Amazon for Workbooks for healing sexual abuse and more!
- **Sacred Sister Circle**: Every Monday at 7am PT, hosted by Tahtahme (the author!) (patreon.com/sacredsistercircle)
- **The Path of a Goddess**: Womb Energy Readings, spiritual information and more. (thepathofagoddess.wordpress.com)
- **Belly Binding**: Postpartum Belly Binding Wrap with Advice (jujusquare.com/en/tahtahme)
- **9 Minds Radio Show:** hosted by Rish De Terra (facebook.com/the9mindsradioshow)
- **Big Liz Conjure Shop**: Rootwork, herbs, incense, classes, and more. (BigLizConjure.com)
- **Hathor's Love**: Waistbeads, feminine statues and art. (HathorsLove.etsy.com)
- **Bohindie**: Waistbeads and jewelry (bohindie.com)
- **Love and Light Healing**: Yoni Steam Kits, Womb Teas, Womb Education (loveandlightheal.com)
- **Manifest, The Wholistic Approach**: Yoni Eggs, Womb Wellness Consultations, Massage Therapy and more (manifesttwa.com)
- **Yoniversity**: Hosted by Truly Kim Morris, you can find affordable, thorough womb learning here. (wombwellnesscenter.com)

If you think you should be on the recommended shops list in future Womb Healing Workbooks, or if you have any suggestions or comments about the Womb Healing Workbooks, please email Tahtahme at thepathofagoddess@gmail.com

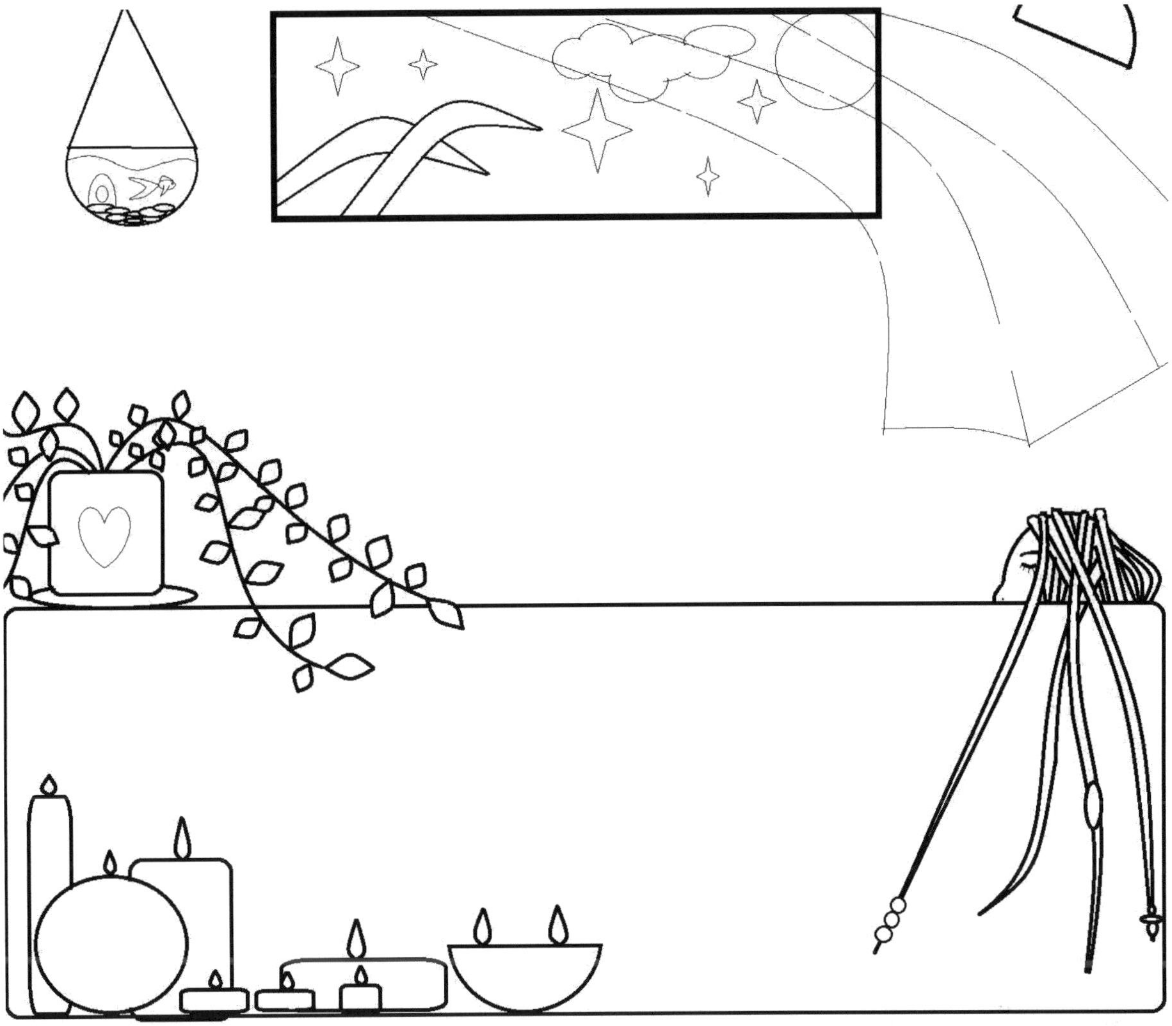

Smoke the room to start the day, all your troubles melt away
Allow the flora grow with care, and this abundance will be shared
Your curls adorn with softest touch, and they shall grow ever much.
Use your crystals every night, allow your dreams to take true flight.
Feel comfort in your melanin; your Ancestors will help you win.

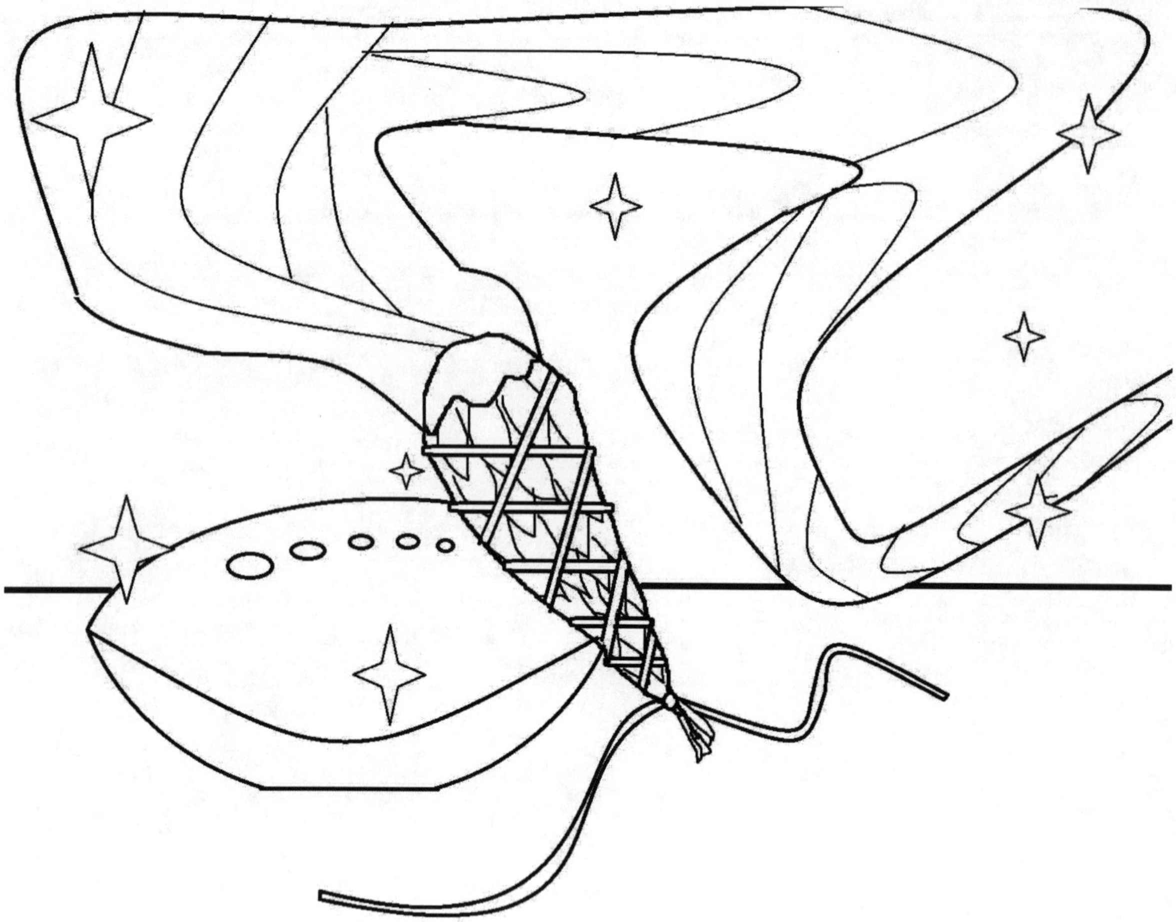

Cherish your punani.

Listen to your womb.

Heed your yoni's needs.

No womb is an island.

A punani in need, is a friend indeed.

An empty womb will clutch at experiences.

No other comes before your punani.

No matter how gold the offering, the pussy is the power.

A womb divided against its body cannot create.

Every clitoris has its day.

Knowledge feeds the punani.

Feed the punani.

Orgasm is an excellent form of defense.

The punani is a temple. The soul decides the worship.

A little of what the pussy fancies, does the soul good.

A punani cannot change the curl of its hair.

The punani is home.

Every honey pot has a sweet spot.

A wet pussy is as good as a dry one to a terrible lover.

One punani is worth a thousand words.

A little of what the pussy fancies, does the soul good.

It's never the honey pot's fault.

A punani shouldn't be a stranger on its own body.

Punani is a beauty. Joy. Forever.

A wet punani lifts all spirits.

A voluntary punani is worth 1000 pressured ones.

A watched punani never creams.

Punani is only punani, but a person is an experience.

Absolute power corrupts a punani.

Better to enjoy the punani you have, than to lust after one you don't.

Your orgasm speaks louder than words.

Better to orgasm once than to never orgasm at all.

Horny pussy always risks it.

The wise womb expects the unexpected.

A womb is never finished creating.

Publicity is good for the punani-- shame is death.

Fuck no punani, hear no lies.

All the world loves a punani that glistens.

Where you grow your hairs, so must you decorate with flowers.

Punani to womb, emotion to reaction, physical to spiritual.

There is no bad punani-- only bad intellect.

Be careful what you manifest-- the womb remembers.

Better to enjoy the punani, than to curse it's burn.

Blessed is the punani.

Pleasure and the punani are equals.

Clean punani is a Goddess Thing.

Punanis find comparisons odious.

The punani always pays.

Happy pussy, warm heart.

All vaginas are desired from a distance.

Do unto your punani what it does unto you.

Don't confuse yoni pleasure with yoni business.

Don't put old news onto new punani.

The way to a punani is through the soul.

Made in the USA
Middletown, DE
10 January 2022

58339548R00222